PEPIE

PEPIE

THE LAKE MONSTER OF THE MISSISSIPPI RIVER

BY

CHAD LEWIS AND NOAH VOSS

FOREWORD BY KEVIN LEE NELSON

ON THE ROAD PUBLICATIONS

Pepie:
The Lake Monster of the Mississippi River

by
Chad Lewis and Noah Voss
Foreword by Kevin Lee Nelson

©2014 On the Road Publications

All right reserved. No part of this publication may be produced or transmitted in any form or by any mean, electrical or mechanical, including photocopy, recording, or any information storage or retrieval system with the permission in writing from the publisher.

The Pepie image is a copyright of Larry Nielson. For licensing, contact: larry@pepinvalley.com

ISBN-13: 978-0-9824314-8-1
ISBN-10: 0-9824314-8-1

Printed in the United States by Documation

On the Road Publications
3204 Venus Ave
Eau Claire, WI 54703
Email: ontheroadpublications@yahoo.com

Cover Design: Kevin Lee Nelson
Layout Design: Terry Fisk

Dedication

This book is dedicated to all the people who have kept the mystery and beauty of Lake Pepin alive.

Table of Contents

Foreword..i
Acknowledgments..iii

History
1 Unearthing a Legend..2
   Chad Lewis
2 A Brief History of Lake Pepin: The Lake of Tears....................6
   Chad Lewis
3 The Tragic Tale of Maiden Rock..10
   Chad Lewis

Serpent Sightings
4 Native American Sightings and Folklore...............................17
   Chad Lewis
5 Pioneer Sightings..21
   Chad Lewis
6 Modern Sightings..25
   Chad Lewis
7 2011 Expedition..40
   Noah Voss
8 2013 Expedition..58
   Noah Voss
9 Other Monsters Seen in the Mississippi River......................81
   Chad Lewis

Theories
10 Misidentification Potentials..92
   Noah Voss
11 Psychological Suggestion: A Willingness to Believe?.........104
   Chad Lewis
12 Is Pepie a Hoax?...108
   Chad Lewis
13 Cryptozoological Potentials...111
   Noah Voss
14 UFO and Alien Connections..117
   Noah Voss
15 The $50,000 Reward for Pepie..127
   Chad Lewis

Final Thoughts
16 A Biased View of Objectivity..132
    Noah Voss
17 Long Live Pepie!..136
    Chad Lewis

Bibliography..139

Foreword
by Kevin Lee Nelson

"A big catfish collided with Marquette's canoe, and startled him; and reasonably enough, for he had been warned by the Indians that he was on a fool- hardy journey, and even a fatal one, for the river contained a demon 'whose roar could be heard at a great distance, and who would engulf them in the abyss where he dwelt.' I have seen a Mississippi catfish that was more than six feet long, and weighed two hundred and fifty pounds; and if Marquette's fish was the fellow to that one, he had a fair right to think the river's roaring demon was come."
—Mark Twain, *Life on the Mississippi*

Where do the monsters live? It sounds like a question a child may ask a parent while being tucked into bed. Folk tales tell us they live in caves, dark forests, and graveyards. Others say they live mostly in attics, cellars, and dark closets. Sometimes it seems like monsters can be found anywhere —even under a bed—but where are they *really* found? According to most cryptozoologists, folklorists, mystics, and legend-hunters, most sightings and odd encounters with monsters occur in locations with one common feature: they usually occur near a border of some sort, whether physical, mental, or spiritual in nature. Such places include bridges, crossroads, and subterranean places, the latter traditionally understood as gateways to the underworld. One could also include sacred and religious sites, as they are often considered spiritual borderlands providing invisible causeways to spiritual realms or the hereafter. Then of course there are rivers, with their ever-changing serpentine paths; places that are neither here nor there, but always flowing betwixt the two.

The interstitial spaces within our landscape are paradoxical places: at once real and imaginary. They are what psychoanalyst Dr. David Winnicott calls the "transitional space" or the "area of illusion." They represent zones of ambiguity, places existing always on the periphery of reality. They are the *places-between-places* that seem to occupy a special place in the human psyche—peculiar locations that exist in two worlds, where normal and rational rules do not apply. According to folklore, trolls are always found under bridges; ghosts are most often reported being heard or seen ascending or descending staircases (the space between floors); pacts with the Devil are traditionally signed in blood at a crossroads—all places on the edge of somewhere else. Some places are known for being particularly infamous for bizarre phenomena. Often they are referred to as 'portals,' 'nexus points,' or 'soft spots' in our reality. John A. Keel, famous UFOlogist and author of *The Mothman Prophesies*, called these places 'window areas,' a place that is marked by long periods of strange sightings and monster reports.

One of the greatest natural boundary lines in North America is the Mississippi River. It separates an entire nation both physically and symbolically. We often generalize places as being, "East of the Mississippi" or "West of the Mississippi," each side having its own distinct geographical and cultural attributes. It is the longitudinal equivalent of the Mason Dixon Line, separating east from west instead of north from south. The name Mississippi is derived from an Ojibwe word *Misi-Ziibi*, meaning "Great River." When Spanish Conquistador, Hernando De Soto, encountered the Mississippi in 1541 he called it *Rio de Espiritu Santo* ("River of the Holy Spirit"), a hallowed pathway for the Divine. "Old Man River," as many call it today, is a vast and winding borderland full of myths and legends, and also serves as a metaphysical demarcation line between land and spirit.

It is perhaps no surprise that people report seeing strange things in its waters and upon its steep bluffs. The Mississippi River is a rich habitat for creatures both natural and *un*natural. It is home to both the Bald Eagle and the mythical Piasa Bird; the River Otter and the phantom steamboat; the Channel Catfish and the creature of Lake Pepin.

In the Lake City, MN area the Mississippi widens greatly creating Lake Pepin, nearly two miles wide and twenty one miles long—a murky no-man's-land bordered by cliffs, hills, and marshes. When boating along its waters one may enter a nebulous territory between two states; Minnesota and Wisconsin, but also the *conscious and subconscious*. It is in the uncharted waters of the mind that one must heed the old cautionary phrase, *Hic sunt dracones* (Here be dragons)!

Kevin Lee Nelson

Acknowledgments

First and foremost we would like to thank Larry Nielson for all of his help with this project and more importantly, for keeping the legend of Pepie alive for all to enjoy.

We would like to pay our respects to those who paved the way for us to do a book on a sea serpent including: Charles E. Brown, Brad Steiger, P.T. Barnum, Charles Fort, Jerome Clark, Loren Coleman, Bernard Heuvelmans, and A.C. Oudemans.

To all the witnesses who shared their stories with us—thank you.

A huge debt of gratitude to our colleagues who joined us on the 2011 Lake Pepin expedition: Todd Roll, Kevin Lee Nelson, and Jesse Donahue.

Thank you to Sarah Szymanski, Shannon Bona, and paranormal expert Terry Fisk for improving this book.

A hot tallow thank you to John Study - Director of Photography with the Sturdy Group, and Damen Shaqiri - sound engineer for Evolv Media for lending their expertise in our hunt for Pepie. These guys are the best in the business, and added Lake Pepin to the obscenely impressive list of paranormal places that they have visited.

Another big thank you to our friend Linda Godfrey. No matter how many times we pester her, she is always up for an adventure.

A very special thank you once again goes out to Jennifer Voss, Nisa Giaquinto, and Leo Lewis.

HISTORY

Chapter One

Unearthing a Legend
by Chad Lewis

In my quest to research and discover mysterious creatures and monsters of the world, I have always held a genuine fondness for sea serpents. Although the oral stories of these water beasties date back many hundreds of years, they came to real prominence during the 1800s. There is something quaint about the idea that many small waterfront towns were thrown into an uproar by the sighting of some giant beast dwelling in their waters. Tales of spectacular sightings would lead to newspaper headlines, which in turn would lead to flocks of tourists, which would inevitably cause more serpent sightings. Nearly every state had multiple serpents living in their lakes, rivers, and streams. But a majority of these legends would inexplicably die out during the 1920s and 30s. Whether people stopped seeing the serpents, or if the media simply stopped reporting on sightings, the legends began to dwindle. Soon, after decades of absence, only a handful of contemporary serpent legends remained. The rest were relegated to nothing more than fanciful tall tales from a time when people were gullible and newspapers were naïve. But not all legends were lost, somehow a few managed to rebuke obscurity and actually flourish in modern times. It was my goal to seek out these legends and explore the mysterious serpents behind them.

For years I traveled the world in search of what was left of the famed sea monsters. I took two expeditions to Loch Ness to search out the infamous Nessie. I scoured Lough Ree in Ireland in hopes of discovering their serpent. I also tracked American serpents in Lake Erie, Flathead Lake, Lake Superior, Devil's Lake and dozens of other lakes, rivers, and streams in my all out quest to locate these still undiscovered beasts. It seems a bit ironic that after so many years of traveling the world in search of serpents, one of the most fascinating sea serpent stories has been lurking right in my own backyard.

Chad Lewis at Loch Ness

Like nearly everyone else, I first heard of the legend of the Lake Pepin monster (affectionately dubbed "Pepie") in 2008, when a slew of media outlets began covering the $50,000 reward that was being offered up by Lake City, Minnesota, business man Larry Nielson. Lake Pepin sits on the Mississippi River and divides the eastern boundary of Wisconsin from the western portion of Minnesota, and both states have beautiful highways that run alongside the entire length of the lake as the river winds its way south. Prior to 2008, I had traveled along Lake Pepin dozens of times, yet I had never heard so much as a whisper of it being inhabited by a monster. After hearing of the reward, I initially thought that it was nothing more than a novel way for a lakeside town to lure in more tourists. With these doubts lingering, I quickly started digging through old newspapers looking to find some historical documentation that would rule out this possibility. The first article I found was a short report from 1871 that touted Lake Pepin as having some sort of creature described as being somewhere between the size of an elephant and a rhinoceros. The article succeeded in convincing me that there may actually be something to the Pepie legend. With the 1871 article in hand, I set out for Lake Pepin to try to unearth more of the mystery. I scoured through the old newspaper archives, spoke with the historical society, and tried to pry open the memory of many old timers, all the while keeping a watchful eye on the lake.

> Lake Pepin, Minn., is infested with a marine monster, between the size of an elephant and a rhinoceros, which moves through the water with great rapidity.

A newspaper article from 1871 touting a monster in Lake Pepin

Over the next two years I made several return trips to Lake Pepin in search of the monster. During this time, I also managed to correspond with Larry Nielson, who was a wealth of information on both the lake's history and the legend of Pepie. Larry had been collecting more recent sightings of the creature from both residents and tourists alike. As a local businessman in Lake City, Larry was well-known and trusted throughout the community, which put him in the prime position to gather stories that publicity shy witnesses may have been otherwise hesitant to share. At the same time that Larry was documenting modern sightings, I was beginning to find additional old newspaper accounts showing that something odd was indeed being encountered in Lake Pepin.

In 2011, after countless day trips to Lake Pepin, Noah Voss and I decided to launch our first official Pepie expedition. We followed up our first expedition with another (more advanced) expedition during the summer of 2013. All of the details, research, findings and lifesaving heroics from both of these expeditions can be found later in this book (see Our Expeditions). It has been nearly seven years since the reward for Pepie was first issued, and I never could have imagined that such a novel idea would all but resurrect a nearly forgotten legend. I take comfort in knowing that after hundreds of years of sightings, the Lake Pepin water serpent still remains just as intriguing and puzzling as it did when the first Native people encountered it. I sincerely hope that no matter what happens, Pepie continues to keep the people near Lake Pepin on their toes.

Chapter Two

Brief History of Lake Pepin: The Lake of Tears
by Chad Lewis

As a lake on a river, Lake Pepin is somewhat of a geological oddity. Lake Pepin owes its very existence not to the Mississippi River, but to the Chippewa River. Sediment buildup from the mouth of the Chippewa River forms a delta that obtrudes into the Mississippi River causing a backup of water, which is Lake Pepin. At roughly 22 miles long and nearly 2 miles wide, it is the largest lake on the Mississippi River. Its sheer size also helps it function as a flowing state border that separates the western portion of Wisconsin from the eastern border of Minnesota.

Mound Builders
The first people to recognize the vast natural resources of the lake were the mysterious mound builders who were thought to occupy the area somewhere between 600 and 1500 AD. Surprisingly little is known about the life, habits, rituals, civilization and beliefs of this first people. Thought to be the ancestors of today's Native Americans, much of what is known has been gleaned through archaeological and anthropological studies of the mounds they left behind. Widely thought to be sacred burial grounds, these raised mounds were often constructed in the shape of an animal or bird, shapes that were easier to decipher from the sky.

History

Little is known about the mysterious mound builders

Native Americans

For generations the Native people lived in harmony with the lake, utilizing its abundant resources for their survival. A series of treaties throughout the early and mid-1800s slowly forced tribes from their lands. In 1830, as part of the Treaty of Prairie du Chien, many of the tribes agreed to land cession—which further deprived tribes of their hunting lands. Many local chiefs were well-respected and looked at as honorable men. Many Native Americans stayed in the area, and local historians tell that, for the most part, they shared peaceful relationships with the white pioneers.

Early Pioneers

For decades before the first permanent settlements were established, Lake Pepin was visited by a series of adventurous explorers, ambitious fur traders, and driven missionaries. Although these excursions were often sporadic and fleeting, they laid the groundwork for the larger influx of white people that would inevitably follow. By the early 1800s, numerous towns started to form along the mighty river. Red Wing, Wabasha, Pepin, Stockholm, Bay City, Reeds Landing, and Maiden Rock all sprung up to suit the needs of the ever expanding commerce brought forth by the Mississippi River.

Sea Wing Disaster

On July 13, 1890 the Grim Reaper paid a visit to Lake Pepin, eager to collect the souls from the worst maritime disaster in the history of the Upper Mississippi. Over 200 passengers aboard the Sea Wing, a 135-foot-long stern-wheeled rafter, were soaking up the beauty of the Mississippi River, unaware that Death was silently lurking nearby. The Sea Wing had set off from Red Wing, Minnesota, on a 17 mile excursion, reaching Camp Lakeview around midday. As the string orchestra entertained, the insouciant passengers enjoyed a mid-afternoon picnic. The Sea Wing was perfectly positioned halfway between Maiden Rock and Central Point. While all seemed just fine, the Sea Wing's ever vigilant captain knew the hot and humid weather could turn the placid lake into a frenzy without a moment's notice. When dark, forbidding clouds soon ushered in high winds, the captain was forced to wait it out. Believing that the worst of the storm had passed, the Sea Wing set off for its return journey, only to discover that Mother Nature had other plans for the ship. The *Milwaukee Weekly Wisconsin* described the severity of the storm, writing, "The whole heavens had been converted into a lighting-lined black canopy of death." The Sea Wing had little chance, the *Centralia Enterprise And Tribune* wrote of what happened next: "A huge wave struck the craft in the side at the same moment that a terrific blast of wind more horribly forcible than the others came up and carried the boat over, all of the people on board, 150 or more, being thrown into the water, some being caught underneath and others

Aftermath of the Sea Wing Disaster

thrown into the waves." Horrified witnesses saw very few survivors floating on the water. According to the *Daily Gazette*, only "a few reached the shore, but the most closed their eyes under water never to see light again." When all was said and done, 98 people met their watery grave on the bottom of Lake Pepin.

Birthplace of Waterskiing

During the summer of 1928, eighteen-year-old Ralph Samuelson stepped into Lake Pepin with two pine boards strapped to his feet, and when his brother Ben hit the throttle of the boat, the sport of waterskiing was born. Samuelson had been experimenting with numerous equipment choices but found that eight foot long pine boards with curved tips worked the best. In 1966, the American Water Ski Association officially reconigized Lake City, Minnesota, as the birthplace of waterskiing.

Today

The winding route of Highway 61 along Lake Pepin is frequently listed as one of the most scenic drives in America, and the superstar attraction is Lake Pepin, which serves as the major economic lifeblood to many of the towns and cities that are lucky enough to dot its shores. Throughout the year the diverse towns along both the Wisconsin and Minnesota shores offer up a smorgasbord of events. The opportunity to attend art shows, waterskiing events, historic festivals, an eagle center, and the home of the *Grumpy Old Men* will satisfy even the pickiest of travelers.

Chapter three

The Tragic Tale of Maiden Rock
by Chad Lewis

Sharing the folkloric spotlight with Pepie is a harrowing tale of sorrow and loss that forever haunts the waters of Lake Pepin. Majestically perched along the Wisconsin shoreline is the 400-foot-high bluff known as "Maiden Rock." It is here that the beauty of the bluffs are forever tainted by the timeless tale of lost love.

Like most good legends, the exact origin of the Maiden Rock story remains somewhat clouded in mystery and speculation. The earliest written account of the tale dates back to 1805. Explorer Zebulon Montgomery Pike recorded the story in his diary, which was published as part of his book, *Expeditions to Headwaters of the Mississippi River.* He wrote: "I was shown a point of rock from which a Sioux maiden cast herself, and was dashed into a thousand pieces on the rocks below. She had been informed that her friends intended matching her to a man she despised; having been refused the man she had chosen, she ascended the hill, singing her death-song; and before they could overtake her and obviate her purpose she took the lover's leap! Thus ended her troubles with like. A wonderful display of sentiment in a savage." Based on Pike's account, researchers contend that the event probably took place sometime around 1800. The tale itself may have faded into complete oblivion if not for being intertwined with the highly noticeable rock formation—essentially ensuring that the maiden's story would live on as it echoed off the lips of each passerby.

History

A postcard featuring Maiden Rock

Much like the story's origin, even general details of the tale have morphed and progressed, while specific details have also been muddled by decades of storytelling. The overwhelming majority of versions tell of lovesick young native woman named Princess Winona (even though natives did not use the term "princess" and "Winona" indicates a first born female) who was smitten with her one true love. Oblivious to her wishes and desires, Winona's friends and family coldly arranged for her to be married off to a man who she despised. Rather than spend her life trapped in a loveless arrangement, the young Winona sought refuge from her pain and heartbreak. Distraught and overcome with melancholy, the maiden rushed to the precipice of the 400-foot cliff and dove off, finally finding relief from her pain as her body smashed onto the rocks below. Other varying accounts have swapped the position of the unwanted lover to that of a Frenchman who vies for the affection of Winona by showering her parents with valuable gifts in an unsuccessful attempt to win Winona's heart. However differing and embellished the legends have become today, the early natives firmly believed that the incident really happened. In her 1849 book, *Dahcotah*, researcher Mary Eastman wrote that the Sioux felt strongly about the integrity of the story and that "they are offended if you suggest the possibility of its being a fiction."

Regardless of all the divergent versions of this lovelorn tale, it makes for the perfect supernatural setting. Some researchers believe when death comes in the highly emotional forms of murders, suicides, untimely departures and bizarre accidents, that it leaves an indelible psychic mark that forever stains the location where the event transpired. These locations of grim death act like a supernatural lighthouse attracting all sorts of paranormal activity. For Maiden Rock, the pain and grief that plagued Winona before her suicide is apparently forever trapped at the location of her death. Almost immediately after Winona's death, supernatural stories started to swirl about Maiden Rock. It was said that when the conditions of the wind were just right you could hear Winona's death song echo off of the rocks. Explorers told stories of catching fleeting images of a spectral native woman perched high atop Maiden Rock only to watch her disappear into thin air. Time only seemed to boost the notoriety of the legend. During a February 1918 interview with the *Missouri Ruralist*, author Laura Ingalls Wilder (who was born in Pepin, Wisconsin) wrote, "I was born in a log house within four miles of the legend-haunted Lake Pepin." Since she was only one year old when her family moved away from the big woods of Wisconsin, Ingalls must have later been told family stories of her birthplace, but her glaring omission of any specific details leaves us to ponder just exactly what haunted legends she was referring to. Residing so close to the lake, the family would have almost certainly been aware of the Maiden Rock legend. The same could be probably be said for the legend of Pepie; the Ingalls family did not move away from Wisconsin until 1868—long after oral tales of Pepie originated, and at least one year after the first accounts of the serpent were printed…leaving plenty of time for the family to get acquainted with the serpent legend.

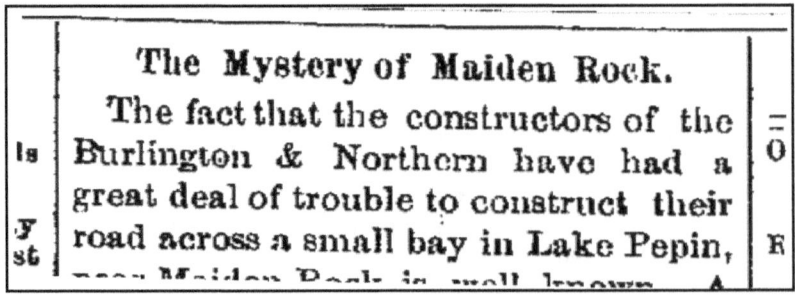

Newspaper story headline from 1887

History

One of the more unique occurrences that only adds to the supernatural reputation of Maiden Rock comes from visitors who are surprised to discover that while visiting the rock they are struck with an overwhelming sense of grief and dread. This uneasy sensation dissipates as soon as they exit the area. Other darker and more sinister legends of Maiden Rock being haunted and cursed by Winona have been circulating the internet for years and function as a dare for curious teenagers looking to test their bravery and impress their less adventurous friends.

Who knows? Perhaps the spirit of Winona is spending eternity at Maiden Rock. Or maybe visitors become swept up by the whole legend and find themselves just a tad emotional during their time at the rock. Regardless of the truth, the legend of Maiden Rock will likely endure for quite some time…and remain as another baffling piece of Lake Pepin's mysterious puzzle.

Serpent Sightings

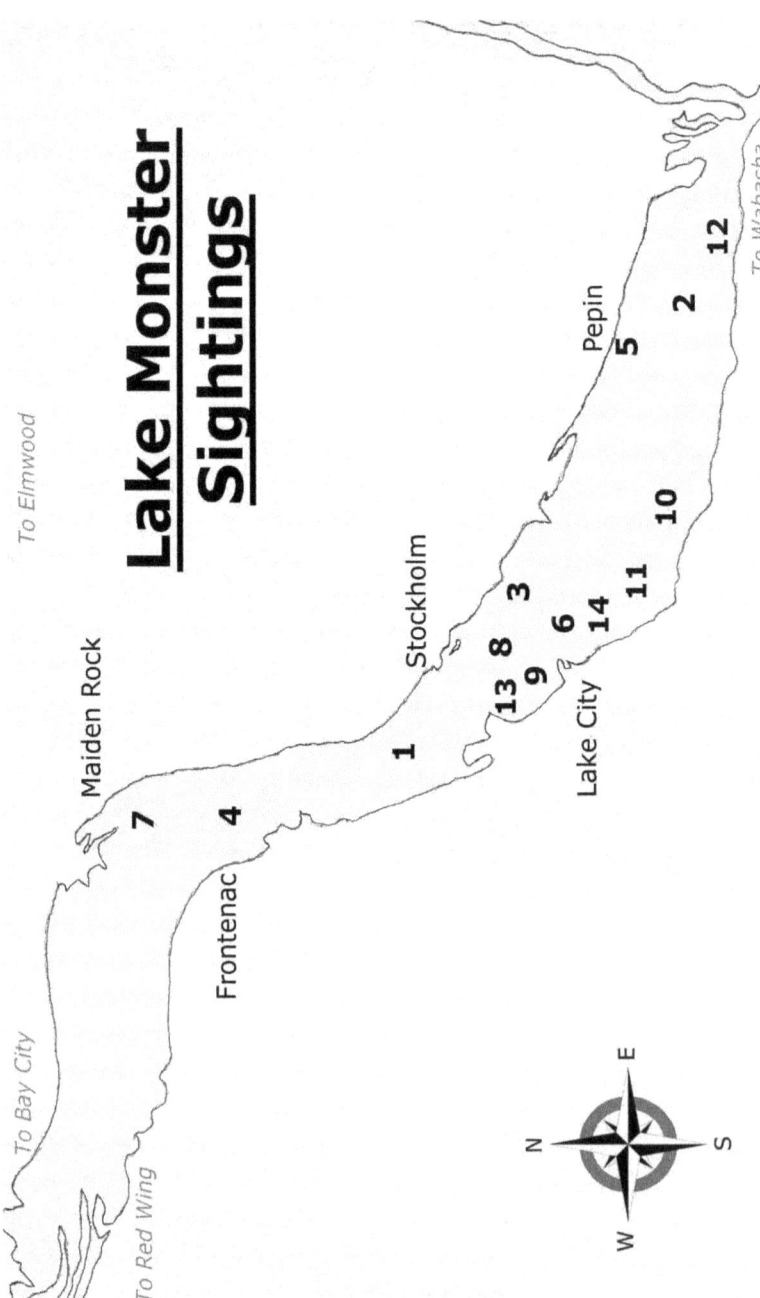

Map of sightings –Corresponding numbers can be located in sightings chapters.

Chapter Four

Native American Sightings and Folklore
by Chad Lewis

One of the main difficulties with researching early Native legends and lore is that nearly all tales were passed down through the oral tradition of storytelling. This poses a great hindrance for researchers looking to critically analyze the stories, rituals, and legends that are all but devoid of any first hand written accounts. Luckily, many early explorers, folklorists, historians, and social scientists began documenting the beliefs, rituals, and tales of the native people, providing a unique insight into many legends that may have otherwise been lost to time.

The absence of any written records has not hampered the formation of a wide variety of Native legends surrounding the history and mystery of the Lake Pepin monster. Creature or not, the Native Americans depended on the lake for their direct survival, making its usage all but essential for daily living. Yet the use of the lake did not come without some trepidation. Perhaps the most often repeated tale tells of the local tribes exhibiting a healthy fear of the lake, due to their belief that something of immense size roamed the waters with deadly intent. Anytime canoes were capsized, tribesman went missing, or unfortunate drownings occurred, many were quick to place the blame squarely on the feared lake serpent. Tribal elders often provided their tribe with the cautionary advice that only the strongest and thickest canoes be used to traverse the lake—canoes which would greatly enhance one's chance of surviving an attack from the water beast.

Legend tells that only the strongest canoes like these would have been used on Lake Pepin

The native people of the Lake Pepin area were not alone in their belief of a giant sea serpent. In his book, *In the Wake of Sea-Serpents*, noted researcher Bernard Heuvelmans writes about the wide spread belief in sea serpents among the Native people, claiming "the Creek Indians, Algonquians, Iroquois, Onondagas and Ojibways believe in a huge freshwater serpent." Native peoples have tales of serpent infested bodies of water that stretch the entire length of the country—including all of the Great Lakes, along with dozens of additional lakes, rivers, and streams. Other serpent tales from tribes throughout the Midwest show that similar serpent beliefs were held by tribes living closer to Lake Pepin. In southern Wisconsin, members of the Winnebago Tribe (Ho-Chunk) believed that a deadly water monster inhabited Devil's Lake. One of their old legends tells of the lake being expanded when the giant thunderbirds who ruled the sky (Wakhakeera) engaged in a deadly battle with the lake's water monsters (Wakunja) that lived in dens buried deep in the lake. The great birds flew high above the land and hurled thunderbolts down at the waters while the water monsters shot up giant rocks and waterspouts from the depths of the lake. Much like Pepie, the monster in Devil's Lake also gained a nefarious reputation as a predator after many tribesman met mysterious deaths on the lake.

Comparable serpent legends also surface from Wisconsin's Geneva Lake. The first white pioneers to the area were greeted with cautionary native tales of a marine monster dwelling in the water. When the white pioneers decided to settle the land around the lake, they discovered several effigy mounds constructed by the ancient mysterious mound builders. Little is known of these mounds builders, as even modern Native Americans have no direct knowledge of exactly who these mound builders were. Effigy mounds are thought to be sacred burial grounds often constructed in the shape of an animal, which could be viewed best from above. Interestingly, one of the mounds near Geneva Lake was designed in the shape of a giant serpent or lizard. Was this effigy mound constructed to create a record of sightings of a mysterious serpent the tribe had actually encountered? Or was it designed for some other unknown purpose? Unfortunately, that question will have to remain unanswered years ago, while the Lake Geneva area was experiencing expanded growth and development, the effigy mounds were removed, thus relegating their possible secrets to nothing more than speculation.

A painting of Lake Pepin Native Americans by Capt. S Eastman published during the 1800s

The widespread prevalence of Native beliefs in sea monsters continued at Lake Pepin, and even if we give some leeway to the possibility of embellishment in the retelling of these legends, the core stories and beliefs seem to be much closer to actual sightings than merely scary stories told around the crackling campfire. Unfortunately we can never be absolutely certain as to just what the Native people experienced along the shores of Lake

Pepin. Was the monster nothing more than a creation tale told to serve as a reminder of the river's deadly strength? Or were these sightings the recordings of encounters with an unknown beast from a people where oral storytelling was preferred over the written word? One thing we do know is that whatever type of beast/myth/monster the Native people believed Pepie was, it continued to make its presence known to the pioneers that began to build permanent settlements around Lake Pepin.

Chapter five

Pioneer Sightings
by Chad Lewis

When the first white explorers visited the area, they quickly became aware of the lake's dark reputation. One of the best known expeditions through the Mississippi was conducted by Father Louis Hennepin, who had been sent, at the request of Louis XIV, to explore New France during 1679-1680. One of the main goals was for Father Hennepin to explore the Mississippi River, making note on its mainly unknown flora and fauna. Father Hennepin may have gotten more than he bargained for at the mouth of the Minnesota River (a tributary of the Mississippi) when he spotted "A huge serpent as big as a man's leg and seven or eight feet long." Upon making it to Lake Pepin, Hennepin noted the abundance of rattle snakes that seemed to thrive in the local conditions. For many decades, Lake Pepin was known as a hot bed of rattle snakes. In their book, *Lake City*, the Lake City Historical Society writes that, according to oral histories, "for the most part, the Native Americans and the settlers of Lake City had peaceful, friendly relationships," which would have provided ample opportunity for the Native people to pass along their sightings and superstitions about the lake monster.

Nearly all of the books, websites, and newspaper articles that reference Pepie mistakenly state that the first published newspaper accounts of the Lake Pepin serpent occurred in April of 1871 (see below). However, many of these mistakes are understandable because, for many years, the 1871

*A 1905 Painting of Father Hennepin at St. Anthony Falls
by Douglas Volk*

sightings were the oldest verified newspaper accounts of the serpent. Luckily, during our research, we were able to dig up a previously unknown Pepie sighting that pre-dated the 1871 case by nearly four years. We are also confident that, in the future, as more and more archives from small, nearly forgotten newspapers around the country go digital, even earlier recorded sightings of the serpent will be found.

August - 1867 (1)
The first known newspaper account of the Lake Pepin monster tells of a party of raftsmen from St. Louis who encountered some unknown aquatic beast while cruising through the lake.

April - 1871 (2)
"Living Curiosity" was the article headline from the April 26, 1871 edition of the *Wabasha County Sentinel*. The article details the story of Giles Hyde and C. Page Bonney, who claimed to have spotted some sort of sea monster in the waters of Lake Pepin somewhere between Wabasha, MN, and Stockholm, WI. They reported that the creature was between "the size of

an elephant and rhinoceros" and even with its great size, it was able to move through the water "with great rapidity." The newspaper added further mystery to the sighting by claiming that the same creature had been "seen on one or two other occasions" as well, although no specific dates or times were given. One main drawback of this time period is their general lack of knowledge concerning the lake and its inhabitants. The absence of scientific research was displayed by the *Wabasha County Sentinel*, in which, during the same article, made the erroneous claim that "the lake is known to be very deep; whales might live in it, but this is not likely to be a whale. The question is, what is it?" It is quite understandable that the paper was merely trying to solve these mysterious sightings using the only tools at their disposal. If they would have been in possession of today's accurate depth charts they would have seen that, with an average depth of around 25 feet and a maximum depth of 60-75 feet, the possibility that the unknown creature in Lake Pepin being a whale, seemed a bit of a stretch. However, previous errors notwithstanding, the newspaper did ask the poignant question of "what is it?"

> Lake Pepin, Minn., is infested with a marine monster, between the size of an elephant and a rhinoceros, which moves through the water with great rapidity.

Newspaper account of the 1871 sighting

July - 1875 (3) (4)

Tucked away, in the middle of a column of local stories from the July 14, 1875 edition of the *Pierce County Herald* rests two amazing accounts of something very odd lurking in Lake Pepin. The article details that "a monster of some kind had been seen in Lake Pepin at two different times within the last few weeks." Strangely, the first sighting of the creature lacks any real description, stating only that it was seen "opposite Lake City." Thankfully, the second write-up is accompanied by a bit more detail. The second sighting took place on Thursday, July 8, as a local gentleman, Mr. Hewitt, and two young boys were guiding their skiff from Lake City to Wacouta. Nearing the halfway mark to Wacouta, the group noticed a "dark, strange-looking object" rise up out of the water. Whatever the beast was, it was big, as the perplexed witnesses watched as it rose up over six feet above the water, where it remained long enough to "be seen distinctly" before it descended back into the safety of the lake.

The above mentioned sightings were also recounted in several other regional newspapers, which ran the original article mostly verbatim. However, at the end of the original story, the *Semi-Weekly Wisconsin* postulated on the creature's identity by stating "an eel, four feet long and weighing five and three-quarters pounds, was recently caught in Lake Pepin."

While the settlers of Lake Pepin may have been better equipped with greater scientific knowledge and tools than the Native Americans, their sightings are no less challenging to decipher. In many ways, the shift in belief that took Pepie from being nothing more than a fanciful Native American superstition to that of a full-fledged unknown creature only highlighted researchers' inability to solve this serpent puzzle. Just as the sightings began piling up and researchers began compiling and analyzing them, the bottom fell out of the research. Following suit with many of its sea serpent contemporaries from around the US, Pepie seemed to have completely disappeared during the early and mid-1900s. If tourists and townsfolk of the 1900s were witnessing Pepie, they were either not reporting it to the media or the media simply decided not to cover it because decades went by without as much as a murmur about serpent sightings. Yet, unlike so many other serpent legends that completely died out and never returned, the second half of the 20th century would see a terrific rebound of Pepie sightings.

Chapter Six

Modern Sightings
by Chad Lewis

Pepie stands apart from the hundreds of similarly described aquatic beasts around the country. Throughout the 1900s, when sightings of other creatures all but vanished, Pepie sightings continued to flourish. Not only have sightings continued through the 1900s, the 2000s saw a rash of new sightings—signaling a Pepie revival that looks to continue the 150-year-old legend for quite some time.

Time of Year
Summer can be a hectic time around Lake Pepin as the lake overflows with excited visitors looking to shake off the long winter blues with some sun filled recreation. On any given day, the lake plays hosts to an extraordinary assortment of expert sailors, water skiers, anglers, million dollar houseboat owners, and the ever-present partiers. It makes perfect sense that many of the modern Pepie sightings occur during this busy season when the lake is inundated with visitors. However, monster hunters should take solace in the fact that Pepie sightings are not exclusive to summer—they also have a tendency to spring up when least expected.

1960s
Some of the most prominent Pepie sightings were said to have occurred during the summer months throughout the 1960s. According to Lake Pepin folklore, the 1960s produced numerous accounts of boaters and water skiers finding themselves face to face with the lake monster. These oft-told tales were repeated by many local residents that I interviewed, not

one of whom could provide any specifics on the sightings. While the origin of these stories remains forgotten to history, their circulation continues to spread with each additional decade of re-telling.

Fall 1980(?) (5)

One sunny fall day around 1980, Wisconsin resident Chuck Stone decided to take his son and daughter out for a little late season fishing. Because they had no boat, the family made their way to a nice rock jetty near the Pepin Marina and set up shop. Looking to catch a few sunfish and bluegills, the family spread out on the jetty with the kids positioned closest to shore while Chuck was out near the end of the rocks. Not long after they arrived, Chuck caught sight of a few birds passing over the water. Without warning he watched a stove-pipe-looking creature rise three feet straight up out of the water, snatch a bird right out of mid-air, and quickly descend back into the lake. Unlike other fish that leap out of the water in an arc to catch prey, landing with a loud splash, this beast conducted its hunt with total silence: straight up and straight down. Chuck had roughly only two seconds to capture a glimpse of the creature before it plunged back into Lake Pepin. In a 2014 phone interview, Chuck told me that he estimated the creature's size to be about 10-12 inches in diameter with a wide open mouth—which made it look like an open pipe. The top portion of the beast was completely flat, leading Chuck to assume that he was seeing the back side of the beast's head. The bright day allowed Chuck to clearly make out the creature's gray skin, which he described as looking like that of an elephant's minus the wrinkles, as it was completely smooth. Chuck didn't have long to contemplate his encounter before he heard the sound of his daughter screaming. Rushing over to her, he noticed two brown water snakes in the lake violently hissing as though agitated by something much more dangerous than the young girl. Having received their fill of action, the family quickly gathered up their things and hurriedly sought the safety of the shore.

Summer 1983 (6)

One beautiful summer Sunday, after the majority of weekend tourists had made their mass exodus out of Lake City, fourteen-year-old Shelly Schimbeno rounded up her brother, Adam, and headed out to the lake for an afternoon of water skiing. Relishing a rare crowd-free day, the siblings were skiing in simple circles around the lake. Adam was in full control of the boat, while Shelly, a nature athlete and avid water skier, was busy enjoying the thrill of the water splashing across her skies. What happened next was so strange that nearly 30 years later it remained clearly implanted in his mind as he recounted the story for the TV show *Monsters and Mysteries in America*. According to Adam, their day of boating was going just fine until Shelly began frantically yelling that there was some type of huge monster in the lake with her. Noticing the fear in her eyes and the unnerving tone of her yells, Adam immediately snatched her out of the water and the pair high-tailed it back to the docks.

In a 2008 interview with the *Rochester Post-Bulletin*, Shelly Schimbeno recalled that she had been casually floating in the water with her skis, waiting for the 16-foot boat to pull her up, when she spotted something very large break the surface of the water. To make the matter worse, the beast was close—real close—and "it didn't look like a fish." In fact, Shelly told the *Pioneer Press* that "it came right up next to the ski boat. It scared me to death. The lake monster was as black as night and longer than the boat." Even though the unknown creature appeared to be swimming away from the boat, she didn't wait around to discover where it was going.

Shelly's face to face encounter with the water beast provided her with a whole new perspective on the lake. A lake she once viewed as a beautiful aquatic playground had been quickly transformed into a place where she almost met her watery grave. From that day on, Shelly vowed that she would never set foot in the lake again—a vow that she has easily kept.

1987 Photo (7)

The *Durand Courier Wedge* published a photo on December 3, 1987, with the definitive headline "Proof Positive" that claimed to be "conclusive proof" of the sea monster in Lake Pepin. The Polaroid photo shows what appears to be a humped creature extending its long neck out of the water as it looms in front of Maiden Rock. In the accompanying caption, the newspaper claimed that the photo was taken by an "anonymous shutterbug while viewing swans in the Maiden Rock Area" and was forwarded to the paper by a "Jean S. Diplodocus" (Diplodocus being a type of long-necked dinosaur) who works with a non-existent group ISENIT (I seen it?).

The dubious photo really piqued my interest. Giving them benefit of the doubt, I contacted the *Durand Courier Wedge* in March of 2014, hoping that they could fill me in on some of the missing details that were beginning to plague the Polaroid photo. I was specifically trying to ascertain the credibility of the photo and whether or not it was posted as a prank. It stretches credulity a bit to think that the paper would post such a controversial photo and quote a source (Diplodocus) without personal knowledge of its origin.

My decision to call the paper resulted in one of the most bizarre series of conversations that I have ever had with a newspaper. The first person I spoke with was the phone receptionist, and when I explained the nature of my inquiry, she quickly informed me that no one at the newspaper would be able to help me out. Over the last 20 years of conducting research, I have interviewed thousands of people, and during this time I like to think that I have developed a sense of knowing when someone is not being completely forthright. Something about the manner in which my call was dismissed out of hand raised some red flags—so I asked to speak with the editor. Not surprisingly, I was told that the editor was simply unavailable, although the receptionist would be happy to relay my message to her. A few days later, after failing to receive a call back, I left a few more messages for the seemingly ever-missing editor, all of which failed to be returned. With the book's deadline fast approaching, I gave one last call to the paper; once again I found myself engaged in a weird game of cat and mouse with the receptionist. This time I was told that because none of the newspaper staff were involved with the 1987 photo, they could not be of any help to me. I found this strikingly odd for two reasons. First, the receptionist had repeatedly brought up the fact that she had been with the newspaper for over 30 years, yet she claimed to have no knowledge of the picture's provenance. Second, I was at least hoping that someone would give me the standard spiel regarding the journalist integrity of the paper but, alas, all I got was complete silence. I finally brought up my reservations with the photo that the newspaper had called "conclusive proof." The receptionist stated that "the photo could be a hoax" before reiterating that the paper wanted nothing to do with this story. Realizing that this conversation was going absolutely nowhere, I made one last play to get a quote from the editor. Without so much as a moment's hesitation, the receptionist told me that the editor would not be available to make any comments. Amazingly, when I asked if the receptionist had the authority to make comments and decisions that would have the editor's name attached to them, she simply replied, "Yes." No wonder they skipped the speech on journalist integrity.

Even though I had also viewed the "Proof Positive" photo with a healthy dose of skepticism, I found myself ambivalent regarding the newspaper's role in the whole event. Several possibilities swirled through my mind.

Serpent Sightings

Assuming the photo is real:
1. The photographer, fearing ridicule and unwanted media attention simply made up an alias to protect his/her identity.
2. The creature (object) in the photo is not that of a sea serpent but more of an optical illusion created by a half-submerged log.

Assuming that the photo is a hoax:
1. The newspaper was an unwitting victim of the hoaxer.
2. The newspaper knew the photo was a hoax and was in cahoots with the hoaxer.
3. The newspaper orchestrated the entire hoax.

Even though I had hit a dead end with the current newspaper staff, many unanswered questions about the photo still swirled in my head so I decided to start at the very beginning. A quick call to the Durand library lead me to Patrick Milliren, a former editor with the *Courier Wedge* in the 1990s, who now works for the *Mondovi Herald-News*—and who also happens to be the Mayor of Durand. He informed me that the "proof positive" photo had appeared in the paper before his time and that he really had no information about it. Yet instead of simply letting the matter go, he went out of his way to track down the contact information of his predecessor who was at the paper during the 1980s. Now with an Illinois phone number in my possession, I felt certain that the mystery of the photo would soon be unraveled. I finally reached Tom Scott at his office at the *Quincy Herald-Whig* in Quincy, Illinois. I knew that asking a lifelong newspaper man about the specifics of one story that appeared over 25 years ago wasn't a blueprint for success, yet a brief explanation detailing my interest and research in the Peppi photo seemed to jog his memory. Scott's best recollection was that the photo appeared in the paper as "a lark" done in "tongue and cheek" that was meant to spark conversation and help promote a Peppi festival in nearby Pepin, Wisconsin. Scott was unable to recall who actually submitted the photo to the paper, but believed that most people at the time viewed it as a fun and quirky event, a "take off" on the Loch Ness Monster. Scott had no knowledge whether the photo was hoaxed or not, but he believed the monster story was made up to boost tourism. The photo and accompanying caption are posted below for you to make up your own mind.

Proof Positive
Conclusive proof of Peppi the Lake Pepin Monster has turned up, as evidenced by this Polaroid photo taken by an anonymous shutterbug while viewing swans in the Maiden Rock area on November 25. The inset is a blowup, grainy closeup of the creature. The photo was forwarded to The Courier-Wedge by Jean S. Diplodocus, who heads ISENIT, an organization dedicated to substantiating claims that a reptilian-like beast lurks in the murky waters of Lake Pepin. Diplodocus said the photo presents "conclusive evidence that Peppi indeed exists and seems to be a creature other than a large carp."

August 2003 (8)

Arguably, no one knows Lake Pepin better than Lake City, Minnesota, businessman Larry Nielson. Since 2005, Nielson has captained the Pearl of the Lake, a 100-foot-long authentic 1800s replica paddle wheel boat that operates throughout the bustling tourist season. Hardly a non-winter day goes by where he doesn't find himself out on the lake, reveling in its beauty. As one would expect, spending such an inordinate amount of time on the lake provides ample opportunity for something out of the ordinary to occur. In fact, over his many years on the lake, Nielson can vividly recall two specific events that continue to remain unexplained.

The first occurred in August of 2003 as he was spending the day out in one of his boats (not the Pearl of the Lake). It was one of those perfect late summer weekdays where the water was as smooth as glass and the lake was devoid of people. With no other boats around, Nielson and his friends noticed a huge wake. It was created by some unseen force as it slowly moved upstream through the middle of the lake. Obviously, something that created a wake three feet high and nearly 200 feet long would've had to have been immense in size, yet whatever was responsible for making the wake remained underwater and undetectable.

Six years later, Nielson once again found himself witnessing another puzzling mystery (see Summer 2009).

August 2004 (9)

In 1996, Steve Raymond left the East Coast and relocated to beautiful Lake City, Minnesota. Lake City, which is a popular fishing destination for anglers, seemed like a perfect fit for a man who had spent much of his life fishing the big waters of the East Coast. As a recent transplant to the area, Raymond wasn't privy to the lake's long history of sea serpent sightings. Eight years after his arrival in Lake City, during the summer of 2004, his ignorance of the serpent legend was shattered by a personal encounter on the lake with something that he simply could not explain.

As luck would have it, in August of 2004, Raymond's wife had just received a new digital camera as a gift from her daughter, and with no use for her old digital camera, she passed it on to her husband. Before heading out the door for a full day of crappie fishing with his buddy, Raymond swung his new camera around his neck. He had been planning to devote more time and energy to his painting projects, and hoped to shoot some photos of his friend which he could use as a reference for his watercolor portraits.

The fishermen loaded their gear into the boat and set off toward central point, where they had heard the fish were biting. Halfway between city point and central point, Raymond spotted what he thought was a large tree floating in the water. In the springtime, a large tree in the water would have been a normal occurrence due to all the debris being pushed down river from the frequent flooding caused by the winter thaw. But this was not spring time—it was August— making the tree's presence very odd. Looking to avoid a crash, Raymond pointed out the position of the tree to his friend who quickly replied, "That's not a tree—it is moving." Off in the distance at approximately 75 yards, the two men caught a closer look at the undulating creature slicing through the water From his vantage point, Raymond could only make out the front portion of the creature, whose long neck and humped body extended a good 20 feet out of the water. Just how much of the creature remained hidden in the water is unknown. While the creature bobbed up and down through the water, Raymond acted

Photo courtesy of Steve Raymond
Mysterious creature spotted by Steve Raymond

quickly—he grabbed his newly acquired camera and snapped off a few shots of the beast before it descended back into the lake, where it disappeared from sight. The whole bizarre incident lasted no more than 10-15 seconds, but even with his limited viewing Raymond was able to make out the creature's coloring; he described the creature in a 2008 interview with the *St. Paul Pioneer Press* as being "greenish, with a cast of "yellow."

The two men remained stationary as they waited for the strange creature to re-appear, but whatever had been lurking in the water had descended for good, leaving the friends baffled by what they had just witnessed. If the men had been familiar with the lake's serpent history they may have forgone their attempts to rationalize what had just happened. As a testament to their complete puzzlement, the two friends chalked up the sighting as just another weird fishing event and continued on with their day of fishing.

Still confused and curious, Raymond's friend began digging around for legends of the lake that might shed some light on their recent encounter. A few days later he called Raymond over to his house and presented the research he had found on Pepie—wondering about the possibility that they, too, had witnessed the legendary sea creature.

In March of 2014, nearly ten years after his sighting, I interviewed Raymond in hopes of gathering more details about his sighting. Immediately, it became evident that he was a seasoned fisherman; while living and fishing on the East Coast, had encountered all types of whales, hammerhead sharks, and nearly every other big sport fish out there. He was convinced that the creature he spotted in Lake Pepin was unlike anything else he had ever come in contact with before. Instead of the creature resembling any known fish, he told me that it appeared to be much more similar to a plesiosaur, or "the green dinosaur that you see on the Sinclair gas stations" (Brontosaurus). The photo Raymond shot does appear to show some large creature-like object with a long neck extending out of the water attached to a thick humped body—the type of beast many would find similar to the Loch Ness Monster.

After talking with Raymond for a while, he subtly hinted that he might (or might not) have additional photos that were taken of the creature during his sighting—photos that he has so far been reluctant to release. Hesitancy to come forward with additional details or evidence is quite common with those who have witnessed something out the norm. Many times witnesses bravely risk their credibility, livelihoods, and their reputation by simply conveying their strange experiences. Luckily, as more and more people bring forward their accounts, the amount of pressure placed on each individual witness decreases significantly. One reason he is reluctant to release more details of his sighting stems from his concern that far too often the creature has been portrayed in a much too dangerous light. It was never his intention to scare people away from the lake. On the contrary, as the owner of a local bait shop and pizzeria in Lake City, Raymond would stand to benefit greatly from increased tourism to the lake. Yet by all accounts, his sighting has flown under the radar; he has repeatedly turned down many of the more sensational media opportunities to exploit the legend of Pepie.

Now, nearly ten years after his sighting, Raymond is still searching for an explanation for what he saw darting through the waters of Lake Pepin. Having never seen anything like it before, or since, Raymond can only wait and hope that someday the mystery of Pepie will be permanently solved.

July 2008 (10)
On July 8, 2008, a motorist was traveling along Highway 61 through Lake City, Minnesota, when something abnormal in the water caught his/her attention. Curious, the driver pulled off to the side of the road in order to gain a better view of what appeared to be a 30-to-40-foot aquatic beast swimming upstream against the steady current. Acting quickly, the driver was able to snap a photo of the beast just before it slipped back under the water and out of sight.

Summer 2009 (11)
Larry Nielson was driving along Highway 61 in Lake City on his way to the docks. Just like nearly everyone else who travels this stunning stretch of road, he found his eyes being drawn towards the lake. Nielson took notice of a large wake coming from what appeared to be a 15-to-20-foot half-submerged log moving through the water. Realizing that the log was actually moving upstream against the strong current, he swung his truck to the side of the road, grabbed his camera, and darted toward the lake for a closer inspection. The whole event only took a few seconds, but by the time he reached the shore he found the lake completely void of movement…whatever had been causing the large wake was no longer visible.

Serpent Sightings

Photo Courtesy of Larry Nielson www.pepie.net
A mysterious sight caught by a passing motorist

Labor Day Weekend 2009 (12)

When Heidi Freier and her crew set out on an expedition to Lake Pepin in early September of 2009, they could not have possibly foreseen the imminent danger that awaited them. As a documentary filmmaker, Freier became intrigued by the lure of the $50,000 reward that had been offered up for the capture of the lake monster, deeming it a worthy new film project. As a self-described armchair cryptozoologist, Freier had always held a fascination with the Loch Ness Monster, so when she heard of the stories of Lake Pepin's monster she jumped at the chance to help solve the mystery. She told *Explore Minnesota*, "The opportunity to do something similar here in Minnesota was irresistible."

Equipped with several boats, diving gear, underwater cameras, sonar, and a sense of adventure, the expedition crew believed they had all the necessary equipment to track down the elusive lake monster. The entire endeavor would be filmed not only for posterity, but to hopefully capture indisputable proof of the monster. A bright, clear day with calm waters provided the perfect backdrop for their sea serpent hunt. The crew had just made their way out to the channel when something large appeared on the sonar. Estimating the object to be somewhere between 30-35 feet in length, whatever the mysterious object was, it didn't resemble any fish cluster they had seen before. Looking to gather a closer inspection of the object,

Photo Courtesy of Larry Nielson www.pepie.net
The ILMPDS Documentary Film Expedition

scuba diver Cory Breault suited up and plunged into the water. As an experienced diver, Breault knew the murky water and heavy current of the Mississippi would provide a formable challenge. Yet, it was the stories passed down from other divers—forbidding stories that told of face to face encounters with the huge fish—that filled him with trepidation. Thoughts of being attacked or even eaten tore at his nerves as he slowly descended into the dark, churning water. After a few minutes, Breault finally reached the deeper area of the channel, yet the water's clarity had improved very little. As he searched for a clear view to gather his bearings, he noticed that the water had taken on an unnerving silence. To make matters worse, a weird sensation started to germinate throughout his body...like some sort of paranormal warning bell. Out of nowhere, a strange ringing noise pulsated through his ears, and at that very moment he detected an unknown black image moving alongside of him. As the object quickly changed direction, it kicked up a forceful current of water. Suddenly Breault found himself caught up in a powerful underwater vortex; it was spinning him around like a top as he frantically fought to make his way to the surface. As Breault struggled below, Freier and her crew—unaware of the battle—caught sight of a large wave moving near their boat. Shown for the very first time on the TV show *Monsters and Mysteries in America*, the video captured Freier commenting on the wave—flippantly stating "It's either

Cory or Pepie…something big." A few seconds later Cory Breault emerged from the water in the opposite direction of the disturbance. Not even waiting to catch his breath he began shouting to his crew, "I've seen it. It's big. It's got to be it. Get me out of this water!" Although he never caught a detailed look at the aquatic beast responsible for causing the vortex, the terrifying encounter left an unforgettable imprint on him. In 2014, he told the TV program *Monsters and Mysteries in America* that going back into Lake Pepin was something he never wanted to do again. Nearly five years after the completion of their expedition I spoke with Freier, who, after all this time, was still searching for any explanation that could shine a light on the creature's identity. Like most witnesses on Lake Pepin, she was left with more questions than answers.

October 2009 (13)

Working at the Lake City Beach Cabana came with some pretty spectacular benefits, the least of which was having a gorgeous lake as your office cubicle. Situated along the shores of Lake Pepin, the small shop rented out canoes, paddle boats, and even offered up pontoon tours of the lake for any boat-less visitors. The small operation was run by Roger Garlitch. As a long-time resident of Lake City, Garlitch was well versed in the local folklore that surrounded the lake, even though he personally viewed the legends with a healthy dose of skepticism. One afternoon, while sitting on the shore with a couple of his buddies, his skepticism would be put to the test. The friends noticed that something was causing a ripple in the water about 30 yards out. At first glance it looked as though a fish was simply skimming across the top of the water—only the "fish" was over 30 feet long. With a large snake-like head, the creature bobbed up and down like a serpent before retreating back into the depths of the lake. In 2009, Garlitch appeared on a segment of the TV show *Life to the Max*. The episode shows him and the host slowly pedaling a paddle boat around the lake while a visibly shaken Garlitch recounts his strange serpent sighting. The fateful sighting did more than alter Garlitch's belief in Pepie—it also changed the way he operated his pontoon tours. For years, he stopped his pontoon tours out in the middle of the lake to allow tourists a chance to take a quick dip. However, after his sighting, he feared that whatever was lurking in the water might pose a real danger to swimmers, so all future pit stops were abruptly halted.

June 2010 (7)
Once again, the area around the Maiden Rock Bluff seemed to be a hot spot for serpent sightings. In 2010, Larry Nielson received a photo from an anonymous source that seems to show some odd creature swimming with Maiden Rock in the background.

Photo Courtesy of Larry Nielson www.pepie.net
This picture seems to show some unknown creature near Maiden Rock Bluff

August 2010 (14)
On one of my expeditions to Lake Pepin, I spoke with a woman who vividly remembered her bizarre Pepie sighting. On August 21, 2010, she and her husband were traveling along Highway 61 when something odd caught her attention. From the passenger window, she gazed out at Lake Pepin and noticed something moving in the water that resembled the long

neck and head of a serpent. Not quite believing what she was seeing, the woman jokingly told her husband that she had just seen something that looked like Pepie. Her husband briefly turned his attention from the road to the lake and spotted the same creature. The couple estimated that—whatever the creature was—it had a neck and head that were sticking a good two feet out of the water. It also appeared that the head was attached to a larger body that was mostly submerged under the water. The sighting only lasted a few seconds, and the heavy traffic on the highway forced the couple to keep moving. It all happened so fast that they were not truly sure if they could believe their own eyes. The couple discussed the possibility that what they had seen was a dead log or other floating debris and, like so many others who have witnessed something strange in Lake Pepin, the couple wrote off their sighting as just another unsolved mystery.

Miscellaneous

Many shop owners in and around Lake City, Minnesota, have placed an "Official Pepie Watch Station" sign in their shop windows. What started out as nothing more than a fun and offbeat way to promote the town's legend has slowly turned in to a beacon for those looking to share their encounters. I spoke with the owner of Treats & Treasures, a favorite downtown shop with tourists, who informed me that throughout the past few years several people have ventured into her store looking to share their personal Pepie sightings. I was surprised to discover that several other local stores were also were frequented by those with a serpent tale to tell. At first these reports served as great conversation starters with the customers, but thankfully many of these stores are now beginning to actually document all of the sightings that they receive.

Chapter Seven

2011 Expedition
by Noah Voss

Adventures…exploits…journeys…or quests: Call them what you will, but there are no travel agents, no how-to guides or thrifty touring websites to educate oneself in this arena. When it comes to dark dangerous excursions into true mysteries, one must hope they survive the education consisting of years of real life experience that can have a steep—if not deadly—learning curve.

Separately, Chad and I both threw off the safe and comfortable shackles of being tourists long ago. Such restraints can be invisible to the wearer in the most reassuring way. Removing yourself from the confines of shopping developments just seconds off the interstate, deciding franchised food is no longer an option, and searching—admittedly for hours at times—to discover that nearly-forgotten motel is a skill that takes years to craft into a most agreeable way of life. Escape from the constant programing can be a very therapeutic, if not an outright enlightening, experience.

But how should I start to recount something so full of potential and wrought with reality-bending experiences? Should I introduce the resumes of those who are normally along on these natural adventures? No, that would use up all the words without giving due credence to those travelers. Perhaps the research that goes into the expedition before we even leave? No, too academic and dry. How about the scientific equipment and metaphysical tools taken along to help quantify data or just to enhance the mystery factor? No, that's the wrong focus for here. So hell, let's just jump in with the adventure!

From behind the helm, Chad's outstretched arm pointed into open water. "What's that?" Perhaps his two excursions seeking the Loch Ness Monster in Scotland have honed his serpent sighting skills.

Todd quickly grabbed one of the five pairs of binoculars nearby and focused in on a mysterious dark, slender silhouette that moved through the water a few hundred feet off our port side.

Todd Roll uses binoculars to identify objects in the Mississippi River

But I'm getting ahead of myself. As any seasoned traveler knows, the trek to the destination is as much the adventure as the destination itself. So let's start at the beginning.

It started differently. I wasn't in control. Thankfully "different and out of control" could decidedly be the theme for our travels. Chad Lewis, author of more than a dozen books on all things unexplained had taken point on putting things together for this legend trip. I knew the basics; we were heading to the Lake Pepin area of Minnesota. We had a boat lined up and would spend Saturday braving the turbulent moods of the great Mississippi River. Why? To search for the infamous Pepie Lake Monster, of course. The earliest documentation by non-native folks we can find is from 1867. The *Wabasha County Sentinel* published the account "Lake monster is seen swimming in Lake Pepin" during the year 1871. Reportedly Giles Hyde and C. Page Bonney spoke of witnessing something "the size of an elephant and rhinoceros." The two witnesses went on to say that it "moved through the water with great rapidity." More reports would ensue, up through recent years. Lake City is located on the Minnesota side of Lake Pepin. Their chamber of commerce has been fortunate enough to secure a $50,000 reward for unequivocal proof of the monster. It seems local business owner and captain of the Pearl of the Lake Larry Nielson kindly put up the reward money. One liberal rule applies: Pepie is not to be harmed. The area had plenty of additional history and legends to explore, including an 1890 maritime disaster. The Sea Wing disaster still remains the worst on the Mississippi River to date. The ferry capsized in a storm and 98 people lost their lives. It is said that not all the wreckage or souls were recovered. For those that prefer lighter fare on their legend trips, waterskiing was invented here in 1922, and Lake Pepin is home to the only working lighthouse on the Mississippi River. Additionally, if you've ever followed "Little House on the Prairie," you may be interested to know that Lake Pepin was visited by Laura Ingalls Wilder and her family on many occasions.

Our quarry, however, would be the safe capture of Pepie or irrefutable proof of its existence. No small task…and some of us even retained a level of optimism.

A friend by the name of Jesse and I headed out to meet up with author and fellow adventurer Kevin Lee Nelson. You may have seen him make appearances on the Discovery Channel's *Mystery Hunters* and *Travelers* and ABC's *Scariest Places on Earth*." Also, he's literally the most feared wand maker west of the Mississippi. It didn't take long to pack the vehicle and head out to pick up Todd Roll, co-founder of Wausau Paranormal Research Society. Todd has been quoted in all forms of the media on his work in the paranormal fields over the last few decades and is a friend to the friendless Romanian Gypsy. We connected with Chad at the monster's lair—Lake Pepin. Even after five hours on the road, there was still plenty of daylight left to use up. So we did.

We packed in an average Friday for the avid adventurer. It began by wandering through a spectral light filled graveyard on the greener side of 2,000 unmarked graves.

Crypt where the bodies were over wintered until the ground was soft enough to dig graves

After interviewing three witnesses, we followed that legend by roaming a dark forest patrolled by a ravenous pack of hell hounds. We braved two bridges guarded by ghosts and spoke with a pair of haunted B&B owners, followed by an hour-long investigation of their inn. Of course, we finished the day filled with more than a few spirits of the liquid libation sort. Throw a couple hours sleep in an aging motel along the shores of Lake Pepin behind us and you've got the classic makings of everything but a tourist. By morning we were ready for a good old fashioned lake monster hunt.

The rising sun brought a round of caffeine, a twenty minute drive, and a handful of power bars. Chad interviewed some of the area chamber of commerce folks regarding lake monster sighting locations. The rest of us were busy bringing up Pepie in every conversation we could start with any willing local. Some new sighting locations plotted on the map, we were off to our sturdy monster-hunting vessel. We arrived at the marina and

Huge mounds of sand flank the Mississippi River with Kevin Lee Nelson in foreground

were greeted by an aged pontoon boat. Embracing the added challenge to our adventure, we secured our gear on the deck and shoved off. Pulling from the safety of the harbor, we were greeted by the wakes from speeding luxury yachts—large and breaking at a solid three feet. Wave after wave crashed against our aging vessel, creating a cold and crisp spray that covered everything. I welcomed the added connection to my surroundings, especially as the temperature climbed into the 80s with humidity not far behind. Adding to the navigation challenge were the behemoth barges tugging their way up the river. They left a continuous wake of four-foot rollers, trying our vessel as it would slowly and ominously lift to the crest of each, only to crash down twice as fast. It was quickly agreed that we would need all 22 feet of our aging vessel to return alive. Well, at least dry.

The army core of engineers worked with the mountainous mounds of sand that towered 100 feet above us on the shores. If one opened their eyes just then, they might be forgiven for questioning the country they were in. An hour and a half later we reached the southern end of Lake Pepin. Our hearts

Serpent Sightings

quickened with the possibility of anything emerging from the lake. Even if for just the briefest of moments, maybe we'd experience something. This had basically been the thought in the back of each of our minds since we first laid eyes on the water yesterday. However, when you get out on the water and it is surrounding you, misting up into the air you breathe, and thrashing the vessel that is the last protector between you and a perilous swim for shore…well, it is markedly different. And, of course, here there be monsters.

This story came from the photographer himself, Steve Raymond. At age 57, he and his "fishing buddy were cutting northeast across the lake." The story and image that was posted on Lake City's website states they were planning "to do some pan fishing near Stockholm, Wisconsin." The story was also picked up by the *St. Paul Pioneer Press* and didn't seem to make the newspapers until four years after the actual sighting. Mr. Raymond said, "Up ahead, I thought I saw a tree, but it wasn't a tree. It was undulating."

A distant log protrudes from the waters of Mississippi River doing its best lake monster impression

Drift wood on Lake Pepin

They moved closer to within "maybe 50-75 yards from it." Then he reported, "I saw at least 20 feet of it out of the water." Mr. Raymond shared great detail often lacking in these sightings, stating, "It was greenish, with a cast of yellow." Thankfully he was quick-witted enough to snap a single picture. Unfortunately, as the story was gaining some attention, he was said to have "misplaced" the original.

We would certainly hold onto our precious negatives should anything of interest show itself. Between navigating our way around the perils that the river threw at us, we discussed some finer points of possibilities. Chad's trips to Loch Ness helped him make the size comparison: "Lake Pepin is 22 miles long and 2 miles wide, Loch Ness 23 miles long and 1.5 miles wide." We all agree this interesting but coincidental at best.

There are no locks or dams in the miles between the marina from which we left and the location where most of the sightings have been documented. This left the very real possibility that if Pepie is even at times a flesh and blood creature there is no clear reason why it very well couldn't be sighted anywhere along our route. None-the-less, arriving at Lake Pepin officially created an entirely new level of anticipation. The energy was high as the water calms. Within moments we had our first sighting. Chad pointed, Todd focused in with binoculars, and I wasted no time raising my camera.

Digital camera in hand I'd already snapped two pictures by the time Kevin responded, "It's starting to look like drift wood. Todd confirmed with the binoculars. "Yup, that's a hunk of wood." The large tree branch floated up and down, riding each passing small wake and wave, creating at the time a fairly convincing swimming motion. Between the many dead fish floating about, ducks, sea gulls, the intermittent piece of trash, and diving birds like the loon, we had our work cut out for us on identifying things sighted. The more unique submerged trees just barely poking through the water's surface only every other wave and countless unique wave formations reveal how a less vigilant observer may half witness something and fill the rest in with subconscious speculation. We all speculated that there may still be more to this legend.

Unfortunately not everyone embraces sighting something unexplained in the lake, as we found with an "anonymous" witness on July 9, 2008. Larry Nielson's website features the report of a "very large creature" that was watched moving parallel to the shoreline. The report estimates the creature to be "between 30 and 40 feet long." The report closes with, "A startled motorist traveling on Highway 61 was able to pull over and get a shot of the 'creature' just as it was slipping back beneath the waves." The image of what looks suspiciously like a lateral wave can also be viewed on Larry Nielson's website.

Kevin Lee Nelson stands watch on the deck of a boat searching Lake Pepin for anything unexplainable

Waves in particular should grab a fair amount of any lake monster investigator's research. There are many naturally occurring wave formations to be aware of. Some potentially misidentified culprits could be unusual standing waves, lateral waves, rouge waves, or combinations of transverse

Serpent Sightings

and longitudinal waves. All these wave types can be manipulated by outside factors such as wind or objects (including lake monsters) causing a myriad of diffraction affects and even additionally stunning visual phenomena. Back on Lake Pepin, our sprits stayed afloat by the youth of the day and the actual possibility of having a serpent sighting, even if our chances were on the skinny side of slim.

This same dance continued the rest of the day; each of us took turns finding something in the distant waters worth further investigation and documentation. Each sighting turned up everything but Pepie. At one point we encountered a school of small fish jumping from the water. An exciting few moments. A few inches in length and silver in color, they reached only a few inches into the air before crashing back into Lake Pepin with a splash. Presumably this is a natural behavior and one that most of us have witnessed on countless other lakes. We killed the engine and hoped there was another cause. Perhaps a hungry Pepie was chasing the appetizers about, causing them to choose the temporary and waterless escape of fresh air.

Cameras rolled, photographs clicked...nothing additional appeared but the return of a placid lake. We drifted silently as long as our patience allowed. Firing up the boat's motor didn't cause a repeat appearance of flying fish, likely Skipjack Herring. The Skipjack is well known to inhibit these waters and often is seen performing this way when chasing down prey. The only slightly off thing was that usually they feed closer to dusk. We moved on to hopefully more perilous, monster-filled waters.

Even if Pepie has not yet been hooked by an unlucky fisherman, other prehistoric monsters have. The bull shark has made itself known as far north in the Mississippi River as Illinois. Not too far from where we found ourselves today. In 1937 a pair of fisherman reeled one in, and many speculate that the bull shark is now as far north as Lake Pepin. Some experts denounce the possibility due to dams that line the Mississippi River, seemingly forgetting about the lock system that always accompanies each. Indeed, it is widely agreed that bull sharks have been documented traveling some 2,500 miles inland through freshwater river ways. The distance to Lake Pepin from the Gulf is significantly less.

It is perhaps less debated that the bull shark is one of the most aggressive and unpredictable species of shark, able to attack in a few feet of water. They can grow to lengths of 13 feet and have been known to hunt in pairs—a formidable foe for sure that uses a classic bump and bite attack. Anyone who has watched *Jaws* has likely experienced at least one swim where their mind snuck away and pictured a giant beast of a shark, mouth opened wide and swimming directly towards them. Indeed the film *Jaws* is based upon real life events that took place in 1916 on the east coast of America. One attack was only reported after a beach goer told ocean side lifeguards that a red canoe had capsized nearly 400 feet off shore and was floating just beneath the water. Upon closer investigation, the lifeguards found no canoe—rather just the bloodied red water from what was left of Charles Bruder, who was barely clinging to life after being attacked by a shark. They rushed him to shore where people fainted upon witnessing his deadly wounds. Six days later there would be at least three more attacks, two of them deadly. What often doesn't get spoke of is that these last three attacks took place in a freshwater creek by the name of Matawan—the shark had swam some 15 miles up, with deadly consequences. I had my own close encounter while swimming in the Mediterranean. I was rather unexpectedly circled by a 4-footer in a very uneasy encounter. More to our current swim in the Mississippi, many scientists today believe that the

Photograph by Jesse Donahue
Chad Lewis (L) and Noah Voss (R) survey Lake Pepin during a 2011 expedition

Serpent Sightings

Photograph by Jesse Donahue
Noah Voss clearing boat propeller of undergrowth during
a 2011 expedition to Lake Pepin

shark portrayed in the *Jaws* film as a great white, was indeed a bull shark! Imagine the feeling of a mysterious bump, followed by a tooth-filled, stabbing pain, as you're drug under the murky waters surface…watching the light above slowly diminish into a reddening darkness. Time for a swim!

We geared up with waterproof photo equipment and dive knives—just in case. Grabbing my life vest I was met with chiding from Chad: "You're not going to swim with that on are you?" I hesitated, knowing that any comment was fair game to ribbing on these adventures. I choose my middle of road words best I could, "I think I might." I did, and several minutes later a winded Chad struggled his way back to the edge of the boat to request a life vest of his own. We swam, (more like floating now) and waited. Eventually Chad, Jesse and I clawed our way back into the ladder-less boat. No encounters with Pepie or the bull shark. We made our way further up Lake Pepin. We toured all the points marked on our maps of sightings either documented by history or by our own interviewing of witnesses. Every local has heard where or knows who may have seen something unusual and we dutifully checked each bay as we motored on. Chad had even purchased a fishing license for the expedition in hopes of drawing to the surface things less than usual. Pairing his pole with the largest Muskie bait money could buy, we all enjoyed the prospect every cast brought.

Sadly, Chad caught nothing that couldn't be explained.

By the time we reached Maiden Rock, Chad and I were ready to tempt fate once again in the name of science and adventure. Despite the natural predator pairs roaming the waters, the potentially carnivorous lake monsters to boot, we prepared. I grabbed my dive gloves and Class V rescuers life vest.

The water was still surprisingly warm. With a little help of some homemade chum, Todd helped us push the limits again in the name of discovering some additional firsthand truths to the legend. The sea gulls swung above us as we bobbed up and down on each passing wave. The gulls—only a foot above—dove to the water's surface well within our reach, making short work of any bait that may have been used. Alas no monsters, no sharks, and no life and limb tale arose from this swim. However, nearby Maiden Rock on the Wisconsin shoreline holds its own haunting history to appreciate. It loomed over us as we took our second shark infested swim, searching for Pepie.

The Maiden Rock oral tradition is said to be passed down in the Dakota Nation. Their legend speaks of one of their own throwing herself from the peak of this very location. It is said the Dakota woman named Winona plummeted to her death. The local urban legend now states that on certain evenings a figure in the mist can be seen repeating her very last steps towards the edge. As I looked up from the water, Maiden Rock towered hundreds of feet into the air above—its structure a sheer rock face and an imposing one.

My thoughts turned to another Dakota legend whispered in this area. Some repeat an oral tradition that clearly advised the observant Dakota to not travel on Lake Pepin in the traditional bark canoes. The warning was given with a tale of monstrous creatures that would destroy the thinner walled canoes. It was only advisable to travel on the monster filled lake with the much sturdier dugout canoe. For those not up on their native canoe construction, this style was literally born of a large tree, chiseled and burnt out until the empty center cavity created, and would hold several persons. Alas, the day was nearing the end. We needed to start plotting our course back to the marina two hours south.

Todd Roll charts the course to the next Pepie sighting location on Lake Pepin

Course laid in, we got underway. We were hopeful that the next hour of making our way back out of Lake Pepin would still hold some mysterious encounter. Cameras were readied and binoculars lifted to eyes. More waves, more debris appeared but still no monster. Even a sighting of the natural and known species of large fish would have been exciting at that point. Sixty feet of water can hold some decent sized fish.

We made our way out of the deepest channel in the Mississippi River towards the marina and, as usual, we were left with more questions than answers.

Photograph by Kevin Lee Nelson
Noah Voss navigates a clear way forward on the Mississippi River during a 2011 cryptozoological expedition

Serpent Sightings

Back on dry land, we made our way toward sustenance.

Todd followed up his usual, "So are there any haunted places nearby?" with, "What do you think about Pepie?" Our waitress, who shall remain nameless, expressed her concerns that the entire Pepie phenomenon "was created by the Chamber of Commerce," implying some tourist-seeking trick laid in secret. We knew different, but never let on.

We strolled by a few haunted locations downtown as directed by our waitress. As we moved along, our discussion covered the obvious holes in the theory she was gracious enough to share as fact. Of course the Dakota's oral tradition certainly predates the Chamber, as well as the numerous reports from the 1800s and early 1900s—unless the conspiracy is multigenerational spanning over a century. Motivations on all sides should be questioned in such investigations. Also, it also becomes additionally complicated investigating modern sightings with evolving technology making it easier for more people to perpetrate hoaxes.

From cerebral banter on the expositions of theory and conjecture apposing one's belief systems, we decided to begin a search for what we thought would be more easily obtainable—absinth. The more normal oddities ensued, such as an overflowing toilet in one establishment that reached the dining room, much to the chagrin of the diners. Thankfully we were in the bar. By the end of the night, and after literally drinking at every bar in town (our last waitress walked us through the list to verify), we realized that a small town may not be the best place to find liquor that was illegal in the U.S. until 2007. We remained absinth-less. Not a huge deal, it was all on a whim.

Back at the motel (the high rollers we are), Jesse and Todd took the two beds, Chad the floor, Kevin the chair, and I the third most luxurious location—the sofa. But not before we rolled a solid B film by the name of *Sharkosaurus…Sharktopolis…Shark-something with a dinosaur reference.* One of those types of movies that is just as fun to watch on mute and invent your own dialog. Thanks to the projector Chad needed for his lecture circuit, we were able to watch the lakeside fitting film in a full 65" on the motel wall.

The sun rose before most would wish. Back on the road, spirits were soon lifted with the first legend. A church in the middle of nowhere was sup-

Lutheran Church purportedly frequented by a phantom congregation

posedly frequented by a phantom congregation. Oddly enough, even though it was Sunday morning, this Lutheran church wasn't even being frequented by a living congregation. Only one other soul showed up inquiring when the church service was.

Serpent Sightings

Chad quickly replied, "We were wondering the same thing." It's just easier this way. Further down the road, and the site of yet another Native American massacre, we found reports of mysterious globes of light moving through the dense forest. A few hundred mosquito bites later, we were back on the road. A tour through Northfield revealed some colorful and deadly local history. Frank and Jesse James attempted to rob a bank here. "Attempted," because the townsfolk were alerted and were able to kill and capture several members of the infamous outlaw's gang. A private tour of an opera house built in 1918 revealed a sorted history of a possible speakeasy and perhaps two ghosts. They have named one ghost Ellen, but between the two they report only playful and mischievous actions. Chairs move on their own, even with someone sitting in them. In addition, people have reported unknown wafting fragrances of flowers and fruit. I was intrigued by the report of someone bumping into "something solid" in the dark, only to find nothing there when a light shown. I moved through several rooms in the dark just to tempt fate. I discovered nothing but an embarrassingly solid door frame. It was past time for lunch, so we adjourned to an old school house—now café—just down the road.

Over lunch we discussed the highlights of the trip thus far, and then moved on to sample a local microbrewery's creation. As we enjoyed a dark porter, the acting squad from the opera house toured the entire restaurant and bar. They stopped, sang, and acted out a small sample portion of their upcoming show. They dutifully handed out tickets and personally requested our attendance. Unfortunately, with a solid six hours road time for the last of us to reach home base, we resigned this legend trip was drawing to a close. Ever vigilant that the travel remained as important as the destination, we kept an eye out all along the old river road before turning inland to rolling bluffs. Sticking to the back roads rewarded us with unique antiquaries filled with dusty books and relics from long forgotten pasts.

As with most adventures, this one left me with the overwhelming sense of anticipation for the next.

Chapter Eight

2013 Expedition
by Noah Voss

August in Wisconsin is many things. It holds a flirty relationship with autumn. Many days leave no mistaking that it is summer with the fair chance for blazing temperatures and plenty of sun. As the month progresses, you get that undeniable and mostly intangible waft of fall. It can come on a surprisingly crisp night, or from a tree starting to turn colors. Often I find it is the shadows whispering to me, embedding thoughts that harken Halloween on the distant horizon. Over the years, I've observed this dance; perhaps it truly is the angle of the sun and how the shadows are cast just long enough to lure my consciousness away from daily stress for the first time in the season.

Thursday
I'm sure I was smirking as I slid behind the wheel of the Challenger, eager to spend a day on the back roads, pushing the mass of metal north. Chad Lewis was heading south; we would meet somewhere around the middle to once again to dive into a monster hunt. I couldn't tell you how many times our destination has been the Lake Pepin area in search of more clues to the Pepie mystery, but this certainly would be the longest expedition yet mounted…stretching over four days. We had a 40-foot houseboat waiting for us and trunks full of gear and provisions fit for any foreseeable scenario.

Noah Voss on the back river roads tracing the Mississippi River north to Lake Pepin

We each brought a few new tools and were energized by the chance to finally use them in the field. One was an underwater dive camera rig that I had spent the last two months designing and building; it was going to give us some great HD video footage from the bottom of the lake—or possibly sink the boat. It wasn't remote controlled but was rather attached to a crank on the boat via a very high tinsel strength cable and that, I feared, could prove to be the dangerous element in the plan. Chad had invested in some underwater sonar equipment that would not only paint a pretty clear picture of objects in the water but also on the bottom…along with valuable data such as water temperature and depth.

After a day behind the wheel, it was evening when we spent outfitting the boat with 12 video cameras and a littering of investigation equipment specific to our task. If Pepie or anything else worth mentioning was going to show itself, we would have documentation.

Beers and bed for a short nap on a stiff bunk. It was great to finally be on the water.

Friday

Morning broke with the familiar anticipation of energy that surrounds the beginning of any hazard-laden adventure. This was a fairly unique experience and one that may have deserved an extra moment to fully appreciate. For example, I didn't play conventional competitive sports growing up, but I did climb mountains. Before one of my last mountaineering expeditions in high school, I got blown off Mount Rainier a few hundred feet below its 14,411-foot summit in a white out blizzard. I still consider it a successful climb, as two climbers and one mountain search and rescue ranger lost their lives to the mountain attempting the same in the days leading up to my own ascent. As with climbing a mountain or actively investigating reports of unexplained mysteries, one must prepare.

Photograph credit USGS
Mount Rainier, Washington State

The dangers can be many and the rewards few, but profound. Not to be overly dramatic, but one prepares in order to increase their chances of survival to a personally acceptable level. That is part of the energy mentioned that an intrepid adventurer faces on the eve of their potentially perilous travels. Now don't be turned off from your own paranormal adventures. They are not all the same, nor do they need to be handled in our limitless approach. As one that regularly pushes the boundaries of generally accepted reality, I've found there is a rather increased need to be aware of my surroundings. We take things to the debatably unhealthy level, and most people don't need to go digging this deeply to have a good adventure. I suppose we're just not most people.

To that point, I've been bait for serial killers while investigating unexplained deaths; scaled cliffs in search of lost ghost towns; singlehandedly orienteered my way through mountain wildernesses in the dead of night on the heels of rumored child abducting cults; spent another night following up leads on a remote mountain in Vermont where at least a half dozen adults have quite mysteriously vanished; and have been told by stone cold faced men that "Ya know, people just disappear when they go looking too far into this UFO stuff." Those are just the exploits I can talk about publically. When you live like this it's within the realm of possibility to make enemies. Those you don't make face-to-face, persons that remain in the shadows of past adventures, can still become aware of you. When it comes time to set out on that adventure, there is always that first step, that moment when there is no more time to prepare and you have to simply hope you've done enough. Not just hope, but completely come to undistracted terms that if you haven't prepared enough, there's nothing you may be able to do to prevent your life from ending. Any river is wrought with dangers, albeit a different set than mountains.

The Mississippi River has a booming commercial lane, complete with behemoth barges stacked 400 feet long, powerful tug boats pushing six-foot wakes behind, undercurrents that can whirl a victim underwater for longer than they can hold their breath, a strong downriver flow that can easily exhaust the most seasoned swimmer or push them underneath countless water obstructions. Of course, if you live in our reality, there are possibly sharks, potentially monsters and when you have enemies, real tangible dangers can follow you anywhere. Keep in mind this is no summer vacation: out for a few hours and then back to the comfortable hotel room. We stayed on the water in the brightest of beating down sunshine and the darkest of damp nights, both awake and in vulnerable sleep. Anything could happen...and frankly that's part of the draw.

It took a few nonstop hours of navigating our way up the Mississippi River until we actually reached Lake Pepin: in and out of the commercial lanes, smashing through five foot wakes that crashed open cupboards and tossed us against walls, traversing around natural shallows and human made wing dams (underwater long stone walls that help manage sediment build up in rivers) that could tear open our hull, quickly sending us to the bottom.

Unfortunately, we didn't have any time to slowly troll our way up the lake to watch for anything less than identified. We kept to our typical, insanely busy schedule that had us pushing the motor wide open to make the scheduled interviews Chad had set up with local historians.

Chad Lewis at the helm during a 2013 cryptozoological expedition to Lake Pepin

As we made our way into the largest marina on the Mississippi River, we were greeted by the Harbor Manager on shore with directions to our slip. It had been some years since my limited time out in the Puget Sound (open to the Pacific Ocean), but Chad skillfully—if not luckily—managed our 40-foot monstrosity around the several hundred thousand dollar yachts. Finally, we gathered up our video equipment and research, we raced up to a crowd of anxious experts on Lake Pepin.

We spent the next few hours speaking with local historians and lifelong residents of Lake City. We drew out every potentially relevant story that we hoped may illuminate something more to this Pepie mystery. Some outright refused to discuss Pepie, while others—with 80 years of life spent not more than a mile from the lake—recalled what it was like growing up with a Lake Monster in their backyard. These first eight people or so that we openly interacted with responded with disinterest, and also with frustration that our focus was not on their perceived beautiful attributes that Lake City offered. Most of this seemed simply born of a sort of indoctrination to growing up with something that most others don't—a lake mon-

Noah Voss pursuing Pepie on the house boat used during the 2013 expedition to Lake Pepin

ster legend. Perhaps a more persuasive viewpoint on this is that the typical American ideology does not widely breed interest in esoteric topics let alone nurture much tolerance for those with them. While most everyone remained pleasant and cordial, I felt a palpable tension likely born of some frustration that we placed our focus on the Pepie legend and not more traditional interests. This is not a new phenomenon for me as an interviewer of countless persons on innumerable mysteries around the world. Truly to each their own and we sincerely thanked everyone over again for their time and sharing their experiences.

Stowing our gear back in the boat, we decided to get back to land. Despite planning for nearly everything, a quick trip to the local hardware store replenished some supplies. As any researcher knows, you don't pass on an opportunity to discover more about your murky mystery. Unfortunately, the good folks working at the hardware store were not able to share anything more about Pepie other than they had heard of the legend.

We were the off for a slightly longer trip to the local pub to recharge ourselves with food and drink.

I was hopeful that the folks bringing us the beer might be more forthcoming by the second round. You see, if you immediately lead with strange questions you are still a complete stranger asking another complete stranger something, well, quite strange. In my experience waiting even that short little while that it takes to drink your first round builds slight, but crucial rapport necessary to reap more from your inquiry. I was confidently hopeful that my seasoned relaxed interviewing skills would begin to pay interest. I feign ignorance. "Isn't there some sort of lake monster legend that was supposed to be around here?" I was again skunked of anything remotely novel. No new information other than a broadening picture of a town filled with folk who are blindly skeptical about ancient lore. The overwhelming impression of Pepie thus far is a community that sees no other option but to toss it in the annals of childish urban legend. This local lore was in actuality built off of documented sightings and oral traditions—dating back conceivably centuries. However, if you had only spoken to the first dozen people that Chad and I had, you would have been left to believe that there was nothing more to Pepie than a modern day scam. What's worse, you would be left to think it was created by one person who thought it into existence only a few years prior. Disappointed that the quest for enlightenment from area residents proved elusive, we made our way back to the shore line. Chad and I took turns listing the facts that flew in

Serpent Sightings

the face of the belief system of so many people we had already encountered. It was disappointing and a little frustrating, but sadly not overly surprising. Beyond that we both cite the oral tradition as recounted by several folklorists and even a possible mention from Laura Ingalls Wilder more than a century before the dozen people we just spoke with completely believed the legend to have been created. No, we would not become dissuaded when all the empirical evidence so far was pointing to something more. We had to, however, acknowledge that this was shaping up to be more of an uphill battle than we had anticipated. Back at the slip, we boarded the boat and shoved off back into the welcoming waters of Lake Pepin.

After a few hours on land interviewing kind townsfolk and washing down the bad news with good beer, we slowly steamed out into Lake Pepin. The day had already given way to twilight, and we still needed to discover safe harbor for the evening's watch.

The assignments marked for the day had now allowed only a short time to troll on the water as we watched for signs of any mystery worth further investigation and a place to weigh anchor.

Long after the sun had sunk below the tree line, we pushed in some calories and caffeine that helped make any monster hunter alert for the 20-hour days. Though our sight was limited through the dark of night, the upper story of our house boat was transformed into a nocturnal monster surveillance deck. With binoculars, still cameras and video cameras all within arm's reach, chitchat and the occasional swigs of beer kept us alert. The only addition to the arsenal of gear from the day were several high powered flashlights that we hoped to soon train on unexplained noises in the dark. Conversation carried from "wouldn't it be great if there were a huge splash and swimming noises headed towards the boat" to more esoteric bantering about exoplanets, as our eyes drifted upward to the ever-increasing number of stars. We kept each other awake by recounting UFO sightings from the area and taking turns climbing down to the galley for the next round. The mysterious splashes never arose and so far as either of us recalled we didn't have any missing time from an alien abduction. Eventually every adventurer must concede that the dawn of tomorrow's investigation beckons so closely that one must call it a day. Indeed, the fact that it was already that day helped to cement the decision. Sometime early Saturday morning we slumbered down to the bunks, battened down the hatches and grabbed a few hours of shut eye.

Saturday

Caffeine and power bars fueled the morning push to motor on to a new Pepie sighting location. The sun was just making its way above the horizon, putting a great angle of light through a thick fog bank on the eastern side of Lake Pepin. Throwing caution to the wind, we set out with Chad at the helm and a northeast heading—hopefully just skirting the menacing fog bank. I had more gear to unpack and construct this morning...namely the good old waterproof metal detector. The pleasant morning on the water with clear skies and comfortable air temperature already in the 60s could create a false sense of safety—we kept a wary eye on the eastern side of the lake still muddled with fog.

We motored further north on Lake Pepin, eyes trained fore and aft for anything worth cruising in for a closer look. Our destination was 22 miles north of where we started yesterday morning when we entered Lake Pepin. No proper lake monster expedition would be complete without surveying the entire lake. Along the way we had the perfect opportunity to investigate each documented monster sighting. First, we needed to drift a bit so we could finish our monster sightings chart.

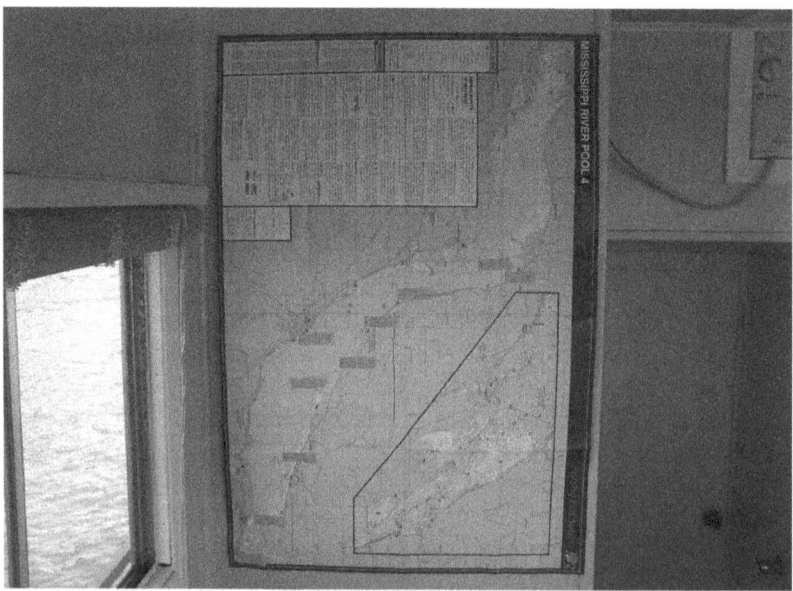

Chart of Lake Pepin marked with numerous Pepie sightings

We had a water way map, coupled with our years of research, and plotted out with likely locations of monster sightings on Lake Pepin. Chad read from our stack of papers, books, folders full of photos, and emails strewn before us on the galley table. As he quoted sightings, I jotted down a few notes referencing each on the small adhesive rectangular papers and stuck them to the map. Those notes keyed us back to more details about each sighting that were tucked away in our stacks of research. Having these sightings charted out helped us on several levels as investigators. Of course, the obvious is that we could look for trends and identify any hot spots for reported sighting locations. Second is that we could more efficiently make note of these sightings as we passed through the same areas. The final point worth mentioning is that we could search for any possible natural explanations for these sightings from the actual area where they occurred. A few hours passed by all too quickly. Relatively calm water was only noticeably broken by the occasionally passing boat heading down river. A remarkably solitary time on such an accepted thoroughfare of a river. It sharply reminds me in the most agreeable manners of all those desolate back roads that Chad and I so often find ourselves drawn to. As expected, the fog bank was dutifully burnt off by the ever rising sun.

Chad and I both took to the second story observation deck to watch. We'd had at least one video camera running the entire expedition; most times we were recording with four. Spying through our high powered binoculars and ultra-zoom digital cameras, we remained vigilant as long as it took us to make our way through an ice cold beer in the blazing hot sun. Already at the northernmost area of Lake Pepin, we continued to gradually drift back down the river and a bit too close to the shoreline. Firing up the boat, we motored south as fast as the engines would push us.

We had set up an interview in Lake City with Captain Larry Nielson of the Pearl of the Lake.

Fog bank rolls across Lake Pepin

We successfully docked back in Lake City, this time just a bit further north of the marina at The Willows private landing. We loved our 40-foot 1970s gritty house boat, but it was dwarfed by the impressive Pearl of the Lake. The boat that Captain Nielson sets out with on scheduled tours and regular charters is an authentic 1800s replica paddle wheel boat, around 100 feet long. During our first chat aboard, I learned that the only means of propulsion are the two independent big red wood paddles at the stern. This would become obvious later that night.

Captain Nielson and Chad have communicated in the past about historic sightings on the lake, and we'd planned to get the latest update—as well as recording his thoughts for our latest Back Roads Lore film episode. He purchased the Pearl of the Lake in 2005 and has since been out on Lake Pepin every day, twice a day during the season. Before that, Captain Nielson grew up not far from Lake Pepin and had spent immeasurable hours here. Our conversation meandered over many concepts, but he was kind enough to start at the beginning. He shared that just after the US Civil War, thanks to newspapers of the time, we know that witnesses watched a "large creature swimming" in Lake Pepin. The Captain's own experiences with unexplained sightings began on a particularly calm day. He recounted watching a long wake from his boat's wheel house, where we now stood. Whatever created the wake was "substantial" (perhaps 300 feet long) and, despite the water being "smooth as glass,"…this two-to-three- foot high wake was moving up river. He speculated that the cause of the wake was under the surface just enough as to not be visible from his vantage point. Captain Nielson continued to share at least two other experiences that left him with more questions than answers, including one from land along Highway 61 that was "12 to 14 feet long" and disappeared just as soon as he had gotten his camera ready. He cleared any confusion by stating that he had witnessed something, but what that something was remains cloaked in the cryptic category of unidentified.

Our spirits lifted by honest, objective conversation around esoteric ideas, Chad and I thanked the Captain for his time and insight. We quickly shoved off in our diminutive boat, re-energized by what another afternoon on the water may bring.

We bore east and motored out into the still secluded lake, on course for 30 minutes. Putting ourselves near a documented sighting location, we cut the motor and just floated in the middle of the widest point of Lake Pepin.

Serpent Sightings

Noah Voss seeking Pepie in the water with Maiden Rock in the background

From here we could observe several documented Pepie sighting locations with the aid of our binoculars and zoom cameras.

We once again returned to the second story observation deck. A couple of chairs sitting next to each other but facing opposite directions allowed us a 360-degree view of the lake. Though we remained diligent in our observations of the water, we sat, nearly relaxed, watching and waiting. Peering often through the binoculars removed any doubt that a passing lateral wave, floating bird, trash or woodsy debris were anything but. Still, each time we spied something there was that moment where we raised the binoculars, half thinking, "What if this is the beginning of an actual sighting?" There was a bit of excitement in that, and it surprisingly didn't wear off easily for two guys whose reality allows for anything. Those moments, unfortunately, were far and few between. We decided to change tactics from static observation to active luring.

We set our new heading towards Maiden Rock. Perched on the Wisconsin side of the Mississippi River, it is a noticeable feature with a sharp and distinctive rock cliff face towering above Lake Pepin. Worth mentioning is that this landmark's own hauntingly spooky history is said to repeat in the evenings when everything is just right. This was the back drop for my first time, this expedition anyway, to hit the water. There would be two times I would be in the drink this voyage and only one of them on purpose. This swim with some gear was to see what we couldn't lure in. It just seems right on a lake monster hunt to get into the water and become one with the environment your quarry would call home. As soon as I hit the water and popped back to the surface, I was instantly happy with my decision to bring my snorkel gear and wear my rescuers life vest. The current quickly pulled me away from the boat at a slightly alarming rate. I've done enough scuba in my life that I felt comfortable putting on my fins in the water. As I floated further and further from the boat, I conceded that it would be nearly all I could do to make it back to the boat had I not opted for the fins. Once on, however, paired with the life vest, I was able to get a noticeable workout kicking my way back to the boat's vicinity. After all, if something chomped me up, I wanted to make sure that I was in frame on one of the many video cameras recording everything around the boat. The current on this expedition was markedly stronger than any of our past outings. What that means for investigating reports of Pepie the lake monster, time will only tell. It was just one of the countless variables that we documented, with the hopes of revealing an illuminating pattern. The dive gear that I adorned allowed me to move a hundred feet from the boat without much worry, beyond getting run over by the occasional faster moving traffic on the lake. For the most part, we had a huge section of the lake all to ourselves for the rest of the afternoon. This allowed Chad a wide and relatively undisturbed area to cast his musky rod, reel and lure...with hopes of drawing something in closer for him or—as he put it—to get me. I left the water after a rumbling freight train snaked its way around the base of Maiden Rock and clanked off into the distance down the river's shoreline. Nothing was taking either of our bait here, and the sun now hung low in the sky. We had to find safe harbor before the dangers of night on the river set in.

Sheltered in a new anchorage, and after at least one round, Chad and I finally got to stop. No more rigging equipment, no more diving in to snorkel against the current, maintaining a solid line of questioning during interviews, or making sure you don't crash your vessel into anything. Just sit and relax. With no more tasks except being vigilant for intriguing noises the rest of the night. Video cameras still rolled, binoculars and cameras were still at arm's reach. The plan was the same as the night before: if anything made a noise, we'd point everything in that direction.

Chad made his way to the bow of the boat on the first floor deck to check a voicemail, and to gain another perspective on the water. I took the opportunity to head to the galley to grab our next round when all of a sudden our CB radio cracked to life. A man's voice calmly requested, "Any vessels on Lake Pepin tonight, this is the Pearl of the Lake...call me on channel six-eight." There was a momentary delay in my reaction as I realized, "Hey, that's us! We're on Lake Pepin." I quickly dialed in channel 68 and heard a boater calling the Pearl. Captain Nielson responded, "Looks like we're pretty stuck on a sand bar and could use someone to make some wakes off our bow." My first thought was, "well hell, we can make that happen." The boater on the CB had a different idea, however, calling back, "Yeah I don't think we're who you're looking for." Before I could jump into the conversation, the Lake City Marina chimed in, asking what the Pearl needed. They were equally unable—or perhaps unwilling—to help, suggesting the Captain contact the fire department emergency rescue. Surprised at the staggering lack of assistance, there was a long enough pause for me to key the mic. I responded, "Ahhh, Pearl of the Lake...this is Noah and Chad on the expedition vessel; we're in your neighborhood. What's your twenty?" Captain Nielson called back, "We're straight across from

Lake City on the eastern shoreline." I key the mic as Chad walked back in from checking his phone. "Ten-four, we are in route. Hang tight." As I looked up from the CB, Chad was already stepping to the helm. I was moving toward the door that exits by the helm area and we both basically said the same thing at the same time: "The Pearl of the Lake is hung up and Captain Nielson needs our help." We were both perplexed and obviously a little slow at putting together how the other person could already know. It turned out that Chad's voicemail was from Nielson, asking if we were still on Lake Pepin.

As adventurers, we often take to treading habitually where most others would not dare wander once. I have found if you continually survive, it seems your reward is a unique skill set, coupled with a life worth living. Chad fired up the engine and I made her ready to set out. Within a few seconds we pulled out from relative safety and into the perilous dangers that lurked everywhere on a river in the dark of night. I ran to our bunks in the aft where we'd stowed most of our tech gear. I tore into my cases, tossing things left and right until I came across two of my dive flashlights. They would have to suffice as we were running dark...I mean hypothetically speaking, we could be. If our running lights were broken—or never actually operating from the get go of this expedition—and we were out at night...that would be in all sorts of violations. Running back from the stern

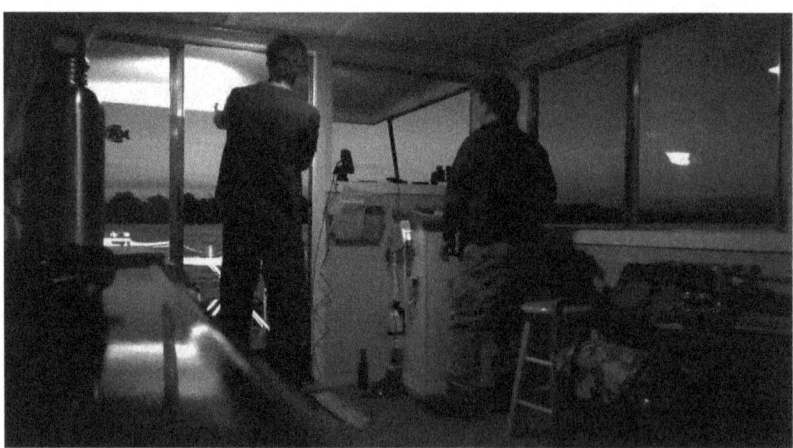

Noah Voss shines a light forward with Chad Lewis at the helm (left to right)

Serpent Sightings

The Pearl of the Lake with the moon in the upper right

to the bow, I turned on all the interior video cameras that I had turned off only 10 minutes prior, just in time to miss things getting interesting. I hurriedly attached about 2,000 lumens to our railings.

Chad pushed the engine wide open as our lumbering boat took the waves and wakes in anything but graceful form—rising and falling, bouncing and thrashing. The night only grew darker and blacker with each passing minute. I again ran to the stern and, with binoculars in hand, searched for some distinguishing light that I could use to help orienteer our way back to the safe haven we had discovered earlier in the night. The dive lights that I procured just for this expedition are newer and thankfully they had a very nice strobe feature that I honestly didn't think I'd ever find a use for. I was wrong. Only a few minutes after we first opened up the motor, Chad and I both found the Pearl of the Lake in our binoculars. There were plenty of lights on the Pearl; she was not hard to spot, but she was a fair few miles from where we were sheltered. The minutes did fly by, and admittedly the excitement of a dangerous adventure really does draw out the best in us both.

While keeping look out for any water born hazards, I spied through the binoculars and reported back to Chad, "Looks like a fair sized speed boat is making laps around the Pearl." This continued for some time as we drew closer. I narrated to Chad again: "Now it looks like they've given up, and The Pearl is still not moving...but wow, is it belching diesel exhaust and those paddle wheels are hummin!" About a mile away, Chad and I could distinguish enough of the situation to hatch our plan of attack. It was a two prong plot: one – don't run into the Pearl, and two – get as close as possible without running into the Pearl. They were laid up on the tricky moving sand bars the Mississippi River likes to throw at even the most seasoned captains. Chad and I agreed that we couldn't go to their starboard side; that would've put us to close to the eastern shore and given us a fair chance of getting get hung up ourselves.

The best chance we had to help them get free was to make a wide-open fast approach to their port side and loop back if the first pass didn't do it to make another shot. That way we could get a magnifying effect with our own wake—the Pearl of the Lake could rise up on those waves. Our 40-foot boat now floated only 300 yards off the bow of the Pearl. We worked north to south with the current, hopeful that our wakes would raise the vessel enough to allow the current and its paddle wheels to pull free of the

Serpent Sightings

sand bar. It was getting darker and more dangerous with each passing moment; the time to act was now.

Using my binoculars, I quickly surveyed the surrounding water from our bow deck for any lurking dangers, and then swiftly shifted over to the helm. Chad and I had been in a few tight situations before…on countless less-than-safe adventures. An understanding, or awareness, forms between fellow adventurers. Where each other's thoughts are during such situations is just known without conveying words. With no more than a meaningful glance between us, Chad opened up full throttle. I moved to our port railing for a better view. We quickly closed the gap and suddenly found ourselves streaking past the Pearl with no more than a 20-foot gap between us. One's mind races in such intense settings. Perhaps because of training and experience, it does not race out of control, but it does race through the flood of data pouring in from heightened senses. We didn't even make it half way down the length of the Pearl before a startling shock swept into my consciousness. Screams!

A crowd of tourists had gathered on the port side exterior deck. To my enjoyment, they had clearly embraced the adventure they found themselves thrust into and were screaming with excitement, booming with exhilarated greetings at our arrival. Our boat punched past. We made a large arch to our starboard side. We found ourselves back to about the same spot we started off at, on the bow of the Pearl…this time only a few hundred feet away. There was no stopping in our plan: the throttle never relaxed. Within a moment, we quickly closed the distance to Nielson's vessel. Brazened by the knowledge gained a moment ago and disappointed the Pearl was not yet free, our trajectory was tighter. The crowd on the upper deck had grown by this time and so, too, had the boisterous cheers that intensified as we moved closer.

The wakes from our second looped arch approach had now reached the Pearl—and us. This was the magnifying effect we were hoping for; however, as our bow passed the Pearl's, port side to port side, we were a mere ten feet apart. Assuredly, Chad saw the needle he was threading from the helm. I watched aft and immediately noticed that our own wake that we were now ridding was leaving little to no room for error. As each of our wakes slammed into our starboard side, we rode it up—only to crash down closer to the Pearl on our port side. We had in effect created three wakes for the Pearl to hopefully use to get free; however, we had three extra, very

The Pearl of the Lake on sand bar

large variables to calculate while moving at a fast rate of speed, treacherously close to another boat and on a swift moving river in the dark of night. I looked up to the crowd that had graciously endeared itself to us just in time to see one enthusiastic tour goer take off his hat and wave it excitedly in the air, much like a cowboy riding a bucking bull.

These paying tourists set out to experience Lake Pepin at the capable hands of Captain Nielson. When they encountered the natural adversity that the environment continually and unbiasedly offered, they embraced it and became true travelers…welcoming of an adventure.

I half smiled—their energy was impossible to ignore—but my focus snapped back to the potentials in the next few seconds. The spray from the huge, red paddle wheels thick in the air towards the aft covered me as we sped beside.

By the time the Pearl's aft and our own passed each other, we were but a few perilous feet apart. We made a second arch looping back toward our starting point; Chad put the engine to idle. We both strained our eyes and watched for any sign of movement with the Pearl. I half exclaimed and half yelled from the bow deck to Chad over the noise of the motor, wind, and paddle wheels pounding the river, "I think she's moving!" The paddles pulled the Pearl of the Lake back off of the diabolical traveling sand bar

Chad Lewis at the helm, Noah Voss on port railing flying by The Pearl of the Lake in the right side of image

and, with the help of the current, she flawlessly righted her route to complete the tour for the passengers. We're happy to report that the tourists didn't have to pay an extra charge for the absolute adventure and story of a lifetime.

The Pearl of the Lake was a striking sight as it moved across the lake, now calm in the night. The charming lights and bright red paddle wheel were reflected in the water, creating a nocturnal shadow that brought a modern—if not turn of the last century—life to the lake. It was a positive energy all around and the atmosphere was comforting. Everything was just right for just a few moments.

Then Chad and I withdrew from our momentary triumph, pointing out the fact that we probably should not spend the night floating in the middle of the lake. Comfort was fleeting with the new task clearly at hand. There was not a moment to waste as we set course northwest. We grabbed our binoculars and searched for some landmarks. Thankfully, I found the lights of our earlier safe harbor, and Chad adeptly held course. The pitch black night pushed us to stay alert for a few more miles.

As Chad and I battened down the hatches again for the evening and made our vessel ready for a few hours of rest, there are rumors of an unintentional swim. That is to say, I fell in the damn water. These rumors may be

The Pearl of the Lake freed from the sand bar by Chad Lewis and Noah Voss returns to port under a nearly full moon

Serpent Sightings

substantiated with two video cameras that half caught the sorted scene, though I'm hesitant to release them in the Pepie episode. You'll have to watch that Back Roads Lore episode to see what I eventually decided; however, here I'll spare you the long drawn out version. Suffice it to say, it did happen fast—one moment I was dry, the next I was completely submerged underwater. I had been very mindful to keep my pockets empty for most of our time on the water, but as it happened my electronic car key (the only one for my vehicle within 600 miles) was in my pocket and my flashlight in hand. I popped back onto the boat and looked behind at the stale, stagnant, growth-covered water I just pulled myself from and decided the best course of action was to sterilize my mouth with some whisky. The first went down so politely that Chad and I followed it up with another, recounting the day's events…making at least one "three hour tour" Gilligan reference in which I called dibs on playing the Professor

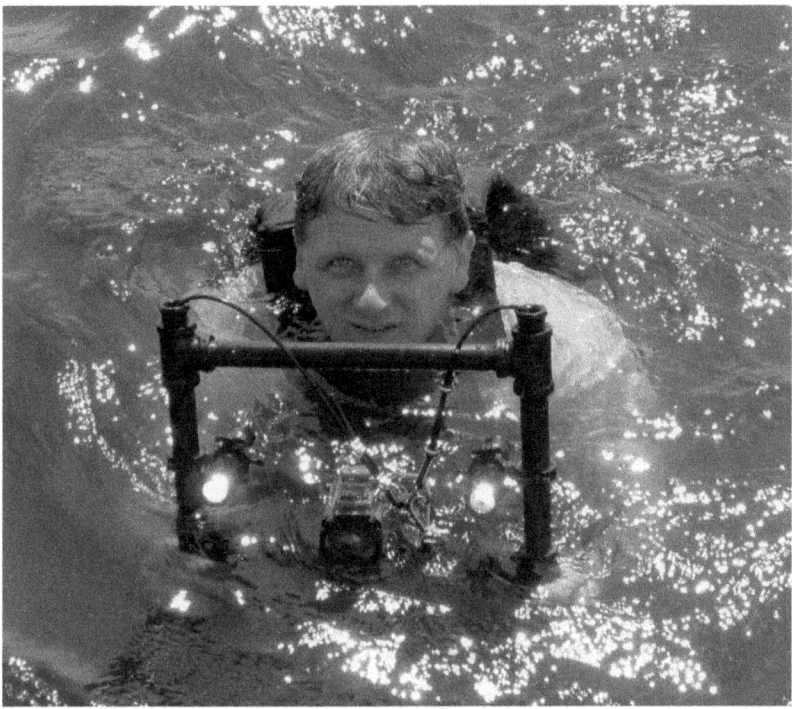

Chad Lewis in Lake Pepin with underwater dive camera rig searching for clues to Pepie sightings

should we ever find ourselves stranded. The night progressed with regular lake watches and some random UFO-watching hours. Conversation slipped into the jocular (we had the Anaconda's film on the in background) and then to that of our usual philosophical diatribe about the global lake monster phenomena.

Late to bunk, early to rise…the life of a monster hunter.

Sunday

Morning came with a few tasks that needed our earliest attention. A broken sonar rig needed a complete overhaul, and I had to swap cameras, pull the flashlights off the boat and attach them to the dive camera rig. Today was the day to get underwater video of Pepie—whatever it is.

Sadly, we were short on time and, as usual, long on plans. We were able to motor about Lake Pepin, checking out a few more monster sighting locations, and got to use the underwater camera rig. Chad even got in the water with the camera rig in hopes of flushing something more out.

We acquired some intriguing footage from under Lake Pepin, but nothing that screamed "lake monster." No time left to finish the last 20 ideas on our to-do list for this expedition, time was our current greatest enemy; we still had at least three hours of navigating our way south down the Mississippi River before nightfall.

We left behind a completely different Lake Pepin than the one we met four days earlier. The water now teemed with human life in all forms, enjoying everything the area had to offer. The traffic was noticeable and slowed our course considerably. Our eyes remained vigilant for anything unusual the rest of the voyage south.

We have yet to be dissuaded by dangers befalling before us when truths are obscured or where danger finds innocence. This adventure was one Chad and I should remember during future days spent researching documents in blasé basement libraries and historical societies and verifying leads from eyewitness interviews…all in the course of digging up new material for the next quest.

Chapter Nine

Other Monsters Seen in the Mississippi River
by Chad Lewis

Standing in northern Minnesota next to a small stream of water flowing through Itasca State Park, it is difficult to imagine that this modest watercourse quickly morphs into one of America's most treasured rivers—the mighty Mississippi. For over 2,500 miles the water twists, winds and turns it way south, eventually pouring into the Gulf of Mexico. Along its storied path lie countless river towns, nearly forgotten remnants of the mysterious mound builders, and the faded ghosts of old steamboats chugging their way up river. Add in all of the various tributaries, and the size and scope of the river becomes the perfect living quarters for hundreds of species of fish, birds and animals. Amongst all of these living creatures rests one of the strangest of them all—the mighty sea serpent (or in this case, the river serpent). While Lake Pepin gobbles up most of the serpent sighting attention, there were a slew of other interesting sightings throughout the entire waterway. During the late 1800s sightings of these aquatic beasts set off a firestorm of controversy; both experts and laypersons alike scrambled to come to grips with just exactly what witnesses were seeing. Skeptics tried to explain away all sightings as misidentifications, hoaxes or complete delusion on the part of the observer. At the same time, those who actually laid eyes on these beasts held firm in their belief that what they saw did not fit easily into any known classification. The following selection of bizarre and unusual sightings showcase the fact that whatever creature Pepie might be, it certainly is not alone!

September – 1877

"A Nondescript Monster in the Mississippi" was the article headline in *the Petersburg Index and Appeal*. Contrary to the headline, the article reported on a very interesting and detailed sighting that took place twelve and half miles south of St. Genevieve, Missouri. Around 2pm on September fourth, a party consisting of J.D. Bradshaw, A.B. Gordon and Louis J. Moran were crossing the Mississippi by boat when they observed a giant serpent stretched out on a sandbar. The group watched the beast for over five minutes as it laid completely still—as though it was merely sunbathing itself. Not content to let the beast rest peacefully, the group fired several pistol shots at it "which seemed to have no effect whatever on the monster, save to frighten it back into the river, where it disappeared, making a strange, horrid noise." Unfortunately, the article omitted many of the key details of the beast's coloring and shape, only noting that it appeared to be around 75 feet in length. Perhaps looking to add credibility to the sighting or to preventively ward off naysayers, the newspaper stated that "one of the gentleman who saw the monster is a Presbyterian elder." It was a common practice for newspapers of the time to include one's social position, community reputation, occupation and/or religious beliefs in order to bolster claims that might otherwise be considered outlandish.

September – 1877

Breaking away from just another routine sighting of the beast, the September 28th edition of the *Derrick* detailed a more harrowing encounter with the marine monster. Like a finely crafted horror novel, the newspaper developed a scary backstory by issuing a warning that all horses and cattle should remain on the safety of land due to numerous reports of the deadly serpent devouring any and all livestock that dared wander into the river. These livestock killings caused "great consternation" among the townsfolk who viewed such killings as direct attacks on their livelihood. Ranchers and farmers cared little about whether the killer was a wolf or serpent; their only concern was how to eliminate the predator. But little did the townsfolk know that it wasn't the livestock that they needed to protect. At approximately 8am on the morning of the 28th, a ferry boat containing two wagons and three horsemen was making its way away from New Madrid, Missouri, to the eastern shore of the river. As the ferry reached the middle of the river, the boat was hit with such a violent shaking that one man was tossed overboard. The newspaper claimed that while the first shake was "like the motion of an earthquake," the second blast "lifted the boat clear from the water and almost capsized it." The water surrounding the boat was severely agitated "as if by a whirlpool," causing huge two foot waves to crash down over the boat. As the ferry passengers were hanging on for their lives, they spotted an "immense object cutting through the water with irresistible force." Although the creature was forty feet away, they could clearly make out the "the pelican-beaked head of the enormous monster" whose thrashing tale was responsible for causing the uproar of water. At the same time, "the leviathan threw a stream of water 10 feet high, making a noise that was plainly heard offshore." Amazingly, the terrified passengers managed to somehow row themselves to the safety of the shore. News of the violent serpent attack spread quickly, aroused the ire of entire town, and lead to the proclamation that an "expedition will be organized here to watch the river and kill the monster." Contrary to most skeptical reports, the witnesses were not some crazy drunks out on a bender. In fact, the complete opposite was true. The newspaper listed the names of all five occupants on board the ferry, claiming they were all "people well known here for their veracity."

October – 1877

On October 18th, the *Memphis Reveille* reported on several sightings of the beast around the Memphis area. Similar to the abovementioned sighting, the paper described the serpent as having "a bill like a pelican, a head like a bull dog, and a slimy serpentine neck and body like a whale." The creature was blamed for "upsetting barges and demolishing rafts"…which only enhanced its deadly reputation.

October – 1877

At first glance, the next story sounds like it would feel right at home sharing the cover of *Weekly World News* with the infamous Batboy. Even though it seems too fantastical to believe, on the off chance that it is not too embellished or entirely conceived of by a newspaper editor, not only

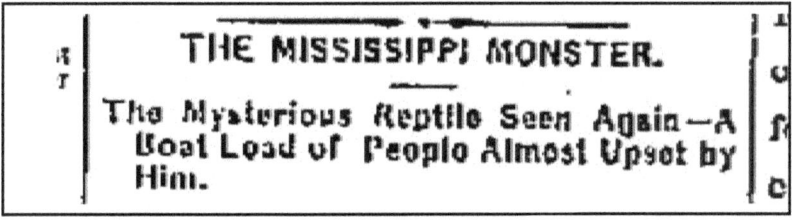

Sensational newspaper stories often stirred up interest in sea serpents

is extremely bizarre, it is also one of the few rare cases of a sea serpent being encountered on land. The story was first told by the *St. Louis Republican* before being picked up by other papers across the country. The case revolves around the family of Mr. Jabez Smith, a "well-to-do farmer on a small scale" living six miles south of Cahokia, Illinois, along the Mississippi. According to the *Indianapolis People*, Mr. Smith was "a gentleman well known in this vicinity as an upright and thoroughly reliable citizen." It was around 4pm in the afternoon when Mr. Smith sent his 12-year-old son, Johnnie, off to fetch a bull that was confined on a pasture near the river. Knowing that the bull could get feisty, Johnnie grabbed a large stick to serve as protection as he cautiously made his approach. He had just entered the pasture "and was flourishing his stick and shouting 'come on,' an invitation the bull seemed unlikely to accept," when suddenly the attention of both the bull and the boy was diverted by loud bellowing coming from the adjoining woods. The guttural noise was "so deep, so dismal and so unearthly that, seized with an awful fright, the boy hurried over the fence on the opposite side of the field." Also sensing the potential danger, the bull "braced in his position with his short tail erect, head lowered, and his hair literally turned forward in the wrong direction from the sudden alarm."

From the edge of the woods the monster made its ghastly appearance in the form of a hideous, large head swaying back and forth on a swivel-like neck that was at least twenty feet long. The head itself was said to be that of "a dog or wolf," complete with "prolongation into a huge bill or horny jaws." The beast was also was equipped with a row of immense fangs, and every time it opened its monstrous jaws it emitted a thunderous hissing sound. Completing the hodgepodge of various animal body parts was the thick "mane of coarse reddish hair" that trailed down the beast's head and neck. Wildly swinging its head from side to side, the beast finally took notice of the motionless bull and began snorting fiercely while simultaneously snapping open its giant jaws in a display of pure aggression. Acting on the threat, "the monster advanced at once and raising its head still higher, it shot forward over the fence and thence came over in swift, billowy undulation, the fence seeming no obstacle at all." The attack finally exposed the rest of the beast's body which could now be distinctly seen. "The great neck terminated in a body somewhat less length, supported upon four short legs armed with immense claws." Weirder yet was the fact that the beast's body was joined to a large bright red tail which had a huge barb at the end. Oddly though, as it lunged toward the bull with its stout body and stubby legs, the beast moved more like that of a snake than something attached to a misshaped body. Amongst a huge cloud of dust the young boy was unable to see any of the action. Instead, the "ground shook as with some internal convulsion" and the "air quaked with a commingled bellowing and roaring" while "there could be heard the snaps of the monster's jaws and the rattling of the bull's horns upon its mauled sides."

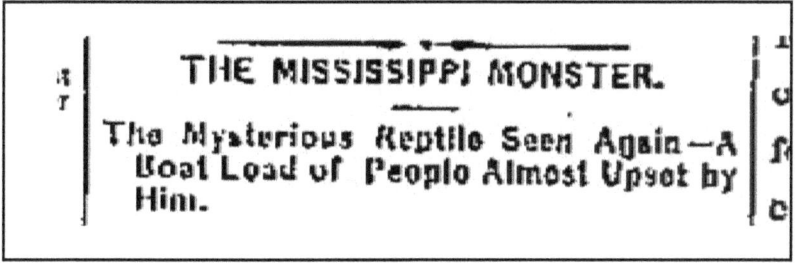

The epic monster battle was detailed in newspapers throughout the country

If the story wasn't already weird enough, what happened next will certainly test even the most diehard true believer. As the tremendous fight was transpiring, the bull was "nearly skinned, with but with one ear and one horn remaining" when the sea monster somehow lodged its barbed tail into a nearby stump, essentially making it a sitting target for the bull's attack. After several charges from the bull, the sea monster summoned up all of its strength and ripped its tail free from the stump. With that, it unfolded its previously unseen membranous wings, "rose into the air like a gigantic bat" and flew off in the direction of the Mississippi. A few moments later the sound of a "tremendous splash" could be heard as though the creature crashed back into the depths of the river.

Finally feeling safe, the young boy emerged from his hiding and began guiding the half dead bull back home. News of the sighting passed from the lips of a neighbor to those of a traveler and finally on to the good people of the *St. Louis Republican* who immediately dispatched a reporter to Cahokia to interview Mr. Smith regarding the events witnessed by his son. Upon questioning by the intrepid reporter, Mr. Smith confirmed that he had visited the site of the epic battle and that he had no doubts as to his son's honesty, claiming, "Ef he told a lie I'd skin 'im."

Needless to say, we must take the abovementioned story with a huge grain of salt, especially considering that the *Shreveport Times* posted a conflicting article claiming that both Mr. Smith and his son not only encountered the monster, but they killed it as well. The supposed monster was said to be well preserved and heading to Shreveport, where it was to be put on display (for a fee).

October – 1877

After the rash of mysterious serpent sightings all along the Mississippi River, the *New York World* proposed the tongue and cheek idea that "the Mississippi river monster, which is described as a sort of half horse, half alligator, and between one hundred and two hundred feet long, be called the "Hippocynophidornithoichthyoides Mississippianus."

January – 1878

After publishing several fantastical accounts of the Mississippi River monster, the *Natches Democrat* still held some reservations as to the credibility of these sightings, stating, "At the time of publishing the above, we felt a little inclined to doubt the monster story, but, now after having ourselves interviewed two gentlemen who have seen it, we really think there is a big sea monster in the Mississippi river." The two gentlemen they interviewed were floating down the river on Captain Ed Baker's produce boat near Island No. 95 (near the town of Lake Providence, Louisiana) when "they were startled by a loud splash in the water." The crew—well acquainted with the river monster legend—was a bit frightened when not more than eighty yards from the boat they witnessed a dark object moving in the water. Without warning, the huge monster began swimming at a fast pace directly toward the boat, making as much noise as a steam boat. As it neared the boat "it turned to the right, striking the stern oar and knocking it overboard." While the rest of the crew retreated to the safety of the cabin, John Coughlin and Dud Kelley had no choice but to remain trapped up on the roof of the boat. From their vantage point, the two men were able to grab a full view of the hideous creature. The beast was 65 feet long, "his body was shaped like a snake, his tail forked like a fish, and had a bill like that of a pelican." From here, the description of the beast get even more bizarre, as the two men claimed its bill was fully six feet in length and that it had a flowing black mane like a horse. Whatever the creature was, when it swam "his head was eight feet above the water" as it moved away down the river. Once the boat docked, the shocked crew refused to leave the cabin fearing that the monster was still out there. The pilot, Mr. George

McCune, had to be lead out by his wife who assured him that the monster had already departed. At the time of this article's printing, the boat remained moored at the local landing, giving even the most skeptical reader a chance to check it out for themselves. Exactly how long the boat was docked is unknown—Captain Barker claimed that it was "impossible to get a crew; as the men think the monster is still following them."

January – 1878

Just above Wilkinson's Landing (near Perry, Missouri) a local man described seeing the huge serpent moving throughout the water. According to the *Perryville Union*, the animal "was ugly looking, its head and mouth being tremendous the latter being something less than the mouth of a cave." Of course the newspaper added some heavy skepticism to the article by claiming "we are rather prone to believe that they are made-up yarns - dished up for the occasion, and should rather see the animal than to hear of it."

June – 1886

The *Anita Tribune* briefly reported that "another river monster" had been spotted in the Mississippi by two fishermen near Muscatine, Iowa. The paper claimed that it must have been a "case of the snakes in its worst form."

October -1903

Fishing on the Mississippi River posed many risks. Outside of the ever changing weather, huge swells, and an extremely powerful undercurrent, anglers also had to be on alert for monster fish that were capable of pulling grown men right out of their boats. That is exactly who happened to William McClain, whose tragic drowning story was published in the *Semi Weekly Iowa State Reporter*. According to his family, McClain took his row boat out on the Mississippi for a day of relaxing trout fishing. "The supposition is that McClain was jerked out of his boat by one of the big

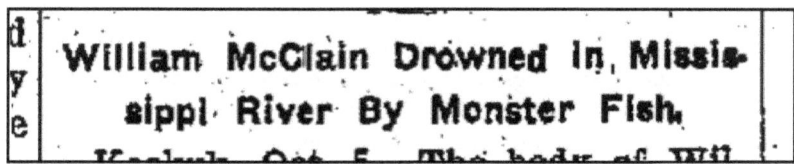

A boating accident caused by a huge fish

river fish which had been caught upon his line, and that when he leaned out over the side of the boat to pull the fish in, the fish gave a jerk which pulled him into the water."

November - 1919

"People Believe There Are Man-Eating Fish in Mississippi" was the headline of an *Altoona Mirror* article seeking to find an explanation for several mysterious drownings that had occurred in the Mississippi River. According to the paper, numerous people around the Hannibal, Missouri area placed "considerable credence in the story that a man-eating fish inhabits the waters of the Mississippi River." The newspaper told the strange story of Carl Tucker, a veteran steamboat worker, who over the years had seen many bodies dredged from the river with mysterious lacerations on the ankles and legs that strongly resembled the "imprint of teeth of some river monster." Adding more fire to the mystery was the case of a 21 year-old woman who, while wading in the river near Hannibal, was heard screaming "oh, my leg" right before she disappeared beneath the surface. Twenty-four hours later, her lifeless body was recovered nine miles downriver. Upon inspection, it was noticed that one of her legs "bore lacerations." As far as we know, these drownings were never officially blamed on the river monster, yet it is interesting to note that a 312-pound catfish was caught within the vicinity of several of these events.

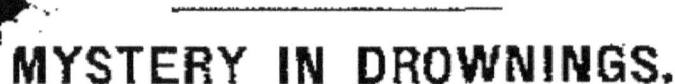

Were these drownings caused by sea serpents?

There was no better time for someone to be a sea serpent researcher than during the mid to late 1800s. During this time researchers had nearly an endless parade of sightings from all over the country. Hundreds of lake, rivers and streams were thought to be occupied by these marine monsters. You could visit any river or lakeside town and easily track down multiple witnesses who were more than happy to share their bizarre encounter. But if the 1800s was the pinnacle of serpent hunting, the 1900s fell from the precipice, as researchers watched serpent sightings from around the country steadily decline, and by the 1930s the overwhelming majority of serpent stories were relegated to the stature of Paul Bunyan and other tall tales. The Mississippi River wasn't spared from the serpent decline either...outside of Lake Pepin it seemed that all of the mysterious creatures (who only a few years prior were causing such great commotion) simply disappeared.

Where did all the serpents go? Did people really stop seeing them, or did the media simply tire of the never-ending sightings and stop reporting on them? It is also not known whether these creatures were native to the Mississippi River or if they wandered in by accident and found it perfectly suited to their needs. In fact, outside of the physical descriptions of these beasts, little else is known or agreed upon by researchers. The list of unanswered questions is limitless. What do they eat? Are they bottom dwellers? Did they travel out into the oceans where scientists classified them as giant squid, oar fish, or numerous other denizens of the deep? Did extinction wipe them out? Maybe the advent of the lock and dam system along the Mississippi trapped them all inside Lake Pepin with no real means of escape. We don't even know how many of these creatures we are dealing with. Due to the varying differences in size, shape, coloring and movement, it seems likely that we are dealing with multiple unknown species—but even that is a wild assumption. And unless it has a lifespan of a few hundred years, there must have been a sizable mating population to continue the species. What we do have are the actual sightings, and even though they might provide no definitive answers, they have spawned the beginning of enduring legend...a legend that looks to keep researchers in search of the truth for quite some time.

THEORIES

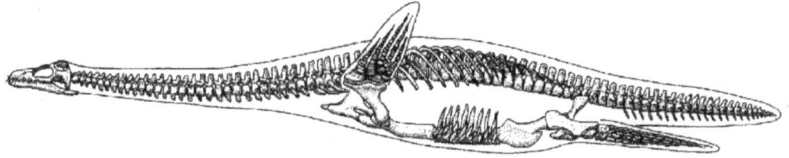

Chapter Ten

Misidentification Potentials
by Noah Voss

Misidentifications happen, and in the waters of something as large and varied as Lake Pepin it is responsible to consider them before we jump to the conclusion of "lake monster." One of the sights most often witnessed on Lake Pepin may be the simple wave or wake.

The creation of a water wave is nothing difficult or obscure. Anyone who has ever been in or on the water has seen this first hand. Animals, boats, and even wind are just a few sources of a wave that then moves across the water, visible at the surface. Lake Pepin has a fair few animals that call it home, loads of boat traffic that move up and down the Mississippi River and, of course, in the widest part of the lake, wind can certainly be a factor. Ignoring for now the mundane windswept boat wake, let's first explore some obscure sources of potential misidentifications.

Physics—the natural science or "knowledge of nature" as derived from Ancient Greek language—encompasses a great many areas of study. Waves propagated through water are certainly a part of nature, studied over many disciplines. Ship designers making the most effective wave-cutting hull, automotive engineers creating the latest gas tank, surface-water hydrologists, physical oceanographers, coastal and marine scientists—all have spent exhaustive hours studying wave phenomena. I searched through these scientists' work for a potential answer.

I read (and reread) countless articles on fluid dynamics covering disper-

Theories

sions of water waves. I studied the water wave propagating sine wave, phase velocity, multi-component wave patterns, and group velocity—whether in shallow or deep water—all the way through to the mathematical formulas. There are many models to choose from...many of them with great visual examples in wave and ripple tank experiments that can reproduce what the mind can imagine. This was not my first, or even second, time diving into this field of research.

My goal was to take in the entire breadth of the subject matter, with hopes of discovering some natural wave formation that might fit at least some of the Pepie sightings. In short, I found nothing that screamed "lake monster," but over the years I have discovered some interesting cases of unusual wave activity born of ordinary occurrences. Waves are a normal feature witnessed on oceans, but they can form when there's no boat traffic or wind on enclosed water basins. These waves are called seiche or standing waves.

For one well-known example, we can look to March 11, 2011. On this date throughout Norway, a mystery had formed. Countless witnesses reported mysterious waves that seemed to appear out of nowhere—nearly five feet high at times. The mystery deepened when it was discovered that the unexplained waves were only witnessed in fjords pointing lengthwise to the northeast. This mystery was solved by day's end, when reports of the devastating earthquake and following tsunami near Japan spread around the world. A documented phenomenon, these seismic seiche waves have even been reported in the famous Loch Ness after the great earthquake of 1755 in Lisbon. Of course, we know that these particular sightings of unusual waves were the direct result of sizable documented seismic activity. Standing waves can also be caused by submarine slides. This natural phenomenon is an underwater avalanche or mudslide, where a large portion of a structure suddenly breaks loose and spills to the bottom. Though submarine slides typically occur in deeper waters than Lake Pepin, they could be a source for some Pepie sightings where nothing more than a wave is observed. However, if we consider this as an explanation, we must keep in mind that seismic seiche waves and submarine slide waves are not known to create one single wave—rather a series of oscillating waves. I could see this phenomena more likely the source of me receiving a report of a phantom boat that could not be seen nor heard...just a ghost boat wake cutting across a lake deep in the dark forest.

Waves are still something that confounds the eye at times. Perhaps it is

*Lake Pepin wave formation as observed during my
2011 cryptozoological expedition*

understandable that a witness who was only half paying attention to their surroundings—distracted by company, piloting their vessel, fishing or a drink—could observe a surface wave interaction and be convinced that it's something more than just water. After all, surface waves on any lake are not simple, nor repetitively soothing. Lake Pepin can have multiple boats putting out varying sizes of wakes...not just interacting with each other, but also experiencing reflection from the ever-changing shape of the lake's shoreline and refracting off of other objects in the water. All of this occurs on a nearly constant basis to the level that it is observable by the human eye. It is a stochastic process that currently gets overrun with variables to the point of randomness, entering the realm of chaos theory. Rare scenarios could theoretically occur, causing a novice passerby to experience something that is like nothing they've ever witnessed before. To go from that unusual wave formation to a lake monster may be a larger leap for some than others. Undoubtedly, this convergence of unique surface wave interactions has been the source for some lake monster sightings around the world at some point in history. This potential "explanation" for some lake monster sightings—including Pepie—does seem to get thin

Theories

when you consider those witnessed by seasoned captains, professional fishermen, and avid boat enthusiasts who certainly clock countless hours on water. Their mental library of wave interactions and the things that can cause them is unintentionally exhaustive, just as a motorist would know many road signs without studying, but merely from regular exposure.

Of course, if Pepie sightings are nothing more than misidentifications of waves, then how could one explain those witnesses who report more than a wake? A couple driving along the Minnesota shoreline of Lake Pepin reported seeing a mysterious creature sticking its head at least two feet out of the water as it moved. Taking the witnesses at their word would have them watching something more than a wave.

A riparian zone is the biodiverse area along a lake shoreline where vegetation and animals blend. Let's explore the native animal species and see if any of those fit well enough to be considered for possible Pepie misidentifications.

The list of native species is fairly large, with around 690 vertebrate species

Photograph by Charles Kennard
The river otter can grow to more than 30 pounds—stretching 42 inches or longer

living in Wisconsin and Minnesota. Looking more closely at the Department of Natural Resources lists of recorded animals, we find approximately 19 amphibians, 35 reptiles and 72 mammals that could be found around or even in Lake Pepin.

Beaver, muskrat, river otter, and mink are just a few semi-aquatic or aquatic animals that most outdoor folks are used to seeing in and around Lake Pepin. Indeed, the United States Geological Survey scientific agency lists Wisconsin's 92-pound beaver as one of the largest ever caught in the world. It was taken from near Lancaster, Wisconsin, about 100 miles south of Lake Pepin on the Mississippi River, and where I spent several years growing up in the wilderness. Most wild beavers in North America tend to average around 45 inches in length and nearly the same in poundage. At those sizes, moving through the water creates a noticeable wake, but nothing that seems extraordinary. What I find noteworthy is the diving and breath holding capacity of many aquatic or semi-aquatic species in the region. The North American river otter has been documented holding its breath for 8 minutes, and the beaver of Lake Pepin region can stay submerged for 15 minutes. Perhaps a beaver observed from a great distance swimming through the water, then submerging, may cause some confusion. Not many people would continue watching for another clue to their unexplained sighting for more than 5 minutes—let alone 15. If we do some fast math with how long a Lake Pepin area beaver can hold its breath

Photograph by D. Gordon E. Robertson
Raft of river otters

Theories   97

(15 min) and how fast they can swim (2 mph), then they could potentially pop up more than 2,500 feet away from their original point of submersion. So, even if a witness watches for 15 minutes, the beaver may not return to the surface within view. If the critter did, not many witnesses would make the connection to what they saw thousands of feet away. It can get even more difficult for our eyewitnesses, when animals crowd together.

A prospective witness might not know that a group of beavers is a colony and multiple river otters are called a raft. Not knowing the grouped names of animals is more than forgivable, but many witnesses may simply believe that certain animals don't band together and exclusively prefer a solitude life style, saving mating seasons. This could lead a witness to theoretically exclude the initial possibility of multiple animals being sighted and misidentified for something monstrous. These animals can't fly out of the water or walk on it, so how can we explore those Pepie sightings that reach out of the water several feet into the air?

The North American river otter has a strong neck that can lift out of the water. Typically, this would be no more than a few inches; even if we gave it a full foot, it wouldn't fit for a likely source of Pepie sightings. Taking a look at the July 1875 lake monster sighting where two witnesses watched Pepie rise up "over six feet above the water," it hardly feels like a river otter misidentification. Another sighting in the early 1980s had an eyewitness watch some monstrous creature lunge three feet up out of the water, using its jaws to snatch a bird during midflight.

Even the very populous white-tailed deer found throughout the Lake Pepin area is known to swim. In 2007, a white-tailed deer was captured on video that had what's called a non-typical antler and what appeared to be another antler growing low or even out the side of the deer's head, nearer to the mouth. This on its own was a sight to be seen; even so, this very unique deer was still clearly identified as a deer in the low quality pixelated video. At a greater distance, and perhaps with multiple deer moving through the water, it is fair to say it would be a confusing sight for most. We just don't have the sightings that would make this fit as a reoccurring misidentification. Were we to, I would suspect many of the sightings would speak to multiple heads and large antlers. I suppose we could speculate that several of any native mammals grouped together, moving through the water in a row, could certainly make identification difficult. This scenario, no matter how unlikely, would still only fit as an explanation for sightings that were made from great distances and for brief intervals. Bearing in mind, of course, that any sighting theorized to be a white-tailed deer swimming would not be able to discount the variable in the sighting where the witnesses state it submerged under the water. Deer don't do this unless they're not coming back up. It stands to be said that Lake Pepin is not the normal environment for deer—or even the random black bear—to be found in.

All of these potentials, no matter how slim, do not accurately explain those sightings that are made at close range, for extended durations, or ones that have details such as green colored scales, or head and neck reaching further out of the water. I use these Pepie descriptions because we have all of these reported sightings with just such accounts of the creature.

So far our research into viable misidentification sources has explored many of the animals living in the riparian zone and even those much further away. To ensure due diligence, let us quickly survey the birds found around Lake Pepin.

Though most agencies agree there are around 408 bird species through the Wisconsin and Minnesota regions, there are a select few that, in my opinion, are better candidates for a misidentified Pepie sighting. Focusing on the aquatic birds that could display unusual characteristics brings us to the loon. At close range, the loon wouldn't be mistaken for anything monstrous other than a chronic red eye. They can dive to depths of 200 feet, remaining submerged for more than a minute and travel more than 1,000 feet underwater. The loon, with its average duck size, leaves plenty of other aquatic or semi-aquatic birds that are much greater in size to be mistaken for Pepie. We can look at the several heron species that can stand a proud four-and-a half feet tall and have huge wingspans of over seven feet. The wood stork, the trumpeter swan, along with the white pelican (to name only a few more) can grow to truly impressive sizes. They, however, are not big on diving beneath the water's surface for any considerable depth or length of time. This rules them out as likely candidates for Pepie misidentifications, especially when none of the enormous number of Pepie sightings contain descriptions of bird-like creatures. That's not to say these birds shouldn't be considered with each new specific sighting of something unexplained in the waters of Lake Pepin. Indeed, everything on the list here—and those that were cut from it—should be held in feasible contention for any Pepie sighting and only ruled out after an objective investigation finds them not fitting. Of course, we have been running down

Theories

the list of wild creatures in the Lake Pepin area that could possibly be mistaken for Pepie. What about fish?

Taking a look at the "Minnesota Department of Natural Resources Section of Fisheries" 2008 report reveals some usable statistics. The section entitled "Angler Survey of Lake Pepin and Pool 4 of the Mississippi River, from 2005 to 2007" documents species and their size at that time. The sampling documented several large species measuring 40 inches in length. Unfortunately, their study doesn't allow for recording of specific lengths over 40 inches, simply stating: 40 inches and above. During our different expeditions on Lake Pepin, we continually saw things in the water hundreds of feet away. Then, by utilizing binoculars, cameras, and video equipment, we were able to easily determine what they were. Upon drawing closer to those that turned out to be hunks of drift wood, we were able to verify that some of the lengths were as small as a few inches. These objects were well under 40 inches and still looked quite unexplainable from a few hundred feet out. None of these things necessarily looked like a lake monster. We just simply couldn't tell with 100 percent certainty what they were. It should also be stated that none of these smaller objects with sizes of a few inches ever looked like they were a few feet to anyone on our expeditions. It did, however, remain difficult to estimate size at a great distance due to the lack of scale and known objects to compare or contrast against. As always, there are more variables to consider when on a monster hunt, such as the 120 different species of fish identified in the Lake Pepin area. Several of the species are very capable of reaching lengths greater than 40 inches. Indeed, northern pike have been caught in the Mississippi River near Lake Pepin that were 53 inches in length (almost 5 feet). Fisherman Tim Pruitt landed a 58-inch blue catfish in 2005, just a state south of Lake Pepin. The fish was 44 inches around the center; it would have made a striking scene if it had ever surfaced. The lake sturgeon is another fish worth mentioning for several reasons. Sturgeons have been pulled from Wisconsin and Minnesota waters at lengths longer

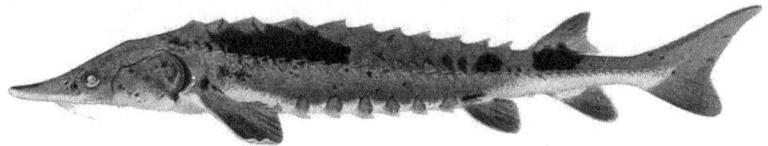

Credit: The Fishes of Illinois by Stephen Alfred Forbes
Lake Sturgeon

than seven feet and more than 200 pounds. Their armored appearance with spiky coverings can create an alarming sight for those not familiar with the fish. The different species of gar and paddlefish that can be present in Lake Pepin only add to the striking fish—some more wild in appearance than most Pepie witnesses may be accustomed. These fish species can also grow to impressive lengths; however they still do not fit for misidentification sources of many Pepie sightings.

No lake monster hunter would be worth their salt if they didn't explore the imaginable misidentification of an eel or lamprey. Even in our northern latitude, the Wisconsin and Minnesota area of Lake Pepin can be home to many different eels and lampreys. Lampreys have a long, classic snake-like shape and can reach lengths of just over three feet long. An impressive sight, but what they make up for in length they lose in girth, having a slender sea serpent sort of shape that doesn't tip the scales at any more than a few measly pounds.

The American eel comes closer to fitting for a misidentified Pepie sighting. They have been documented to grow to nearly six feet in length, though typically they are much shorter in these northern latitudes. With their slender snake-like shape they, too, only tip the scale a few pounds more than the lampreys might.

Of course, snakes should be researched and compared to any past or future Pepie sightings. If we look at the largest naturally found snake in

Credit: Illustration by Ellen Edmonson and Hugh Chrisp for the New York Biological Survey
American Eel

Theories

the Lake Pepin area, we'd find the bullsnake. The largest specimen ever recorded was eight feet, four inches long and would have weighed around 10 pounds. The bullsnake is not a true aquatic snake and would not habitually be found swimming, though they have certainly been known to swim. Typically, the Lake Pepin area bullsnake would grow to no more than around six feet long under average circumstances. The bullsnake, however, is likely capable of getting longer than any lamprey, freshwater eel or even other mammals such as the beaver or river otter…making it a fair contender for a misidentified lake monster. A snake, however, typically creates a much different wake than a large beaver might—and a sizably smaller one. These mundane creatures of Lake Pepin may seem like a practical explanation to some; however, time and time again they just don't seem to match what witnesses have reported when each sighting is taken as a whole.

In 2004, a husband and wife watched something unexplained undulating on the surface of Lake Pepin. They estimated it to be 20 feet in length before it dove once more beneath the surface. In 2009, a group searching for Pepie witnessed a sonar return a reading of 30-35 feet in length and an underwater sighting of something they couldn't explain.

On my own travels to Lake Pepin investigating Pepie, Lake Erie searching for Bessie, Lake Champlain watching for Champ, and even flying briefly through the Bermuda Triangle, I often thought that turtles could make a striking lake monster sight if witnessed at just the right time. Lake Pepin can be home to snapping turtles, likely the area's largest turtle species. The common snapping turtle typically tops out around 20 inches in length and perhaps 35 pounds. Larger specimens in the wild have been reported (but unsubstantiated) reaching 75 pounds. A turtle this size, if fully surfaced, would certainly be noticeable from some distance. A turtle's normal behavior, however, is to remain as submerged as possible while extending its nose to breath, its shell remaining beneath the water's surface. The alligator snapping turtle's normal habitable range is just south of Lake Pepin, but its appearance is much more monstrous—complete with pointed ridges on its shell.

*Credit: illustration from Holbrook's North American Herpetology—1842
Alligator snapping turtle*

Both of these snapping turtles have been known to reach hundreds of pounds in captivity—a marked increase to their wild 35 pounds. Watching one of these promising behemoths glide under your small canoe in the murky waters of the Mississippi River would be unnerving to the most seasoned of travelers. While an abnormally large turtle should be entertained as a thinkable misidentification for Pepie, their likely smaller sizes, when paired with their normal habitat range and innate behavior in the wild, just doesn't make them a very good fit for most Pepie reports.

Theories

Moving past the living creatures naturally found around Lake Pepin, we should also examine inanimate objects. Lake Pepin is on a river and has a current that can, and does, naturally move many things that find their way into its sometimes swift waters. Small drift wood and large logs work their way free from the shoreline as the water levels rise and fall each season. Trash and debris either dumped or dropped into the water can continue for great distances on the surface or just below, bobbing and bouncing with each changing influence. Regarding the possibility of a witness misidentifying something like this for Pepie, the reader must become their own guide in reason and possibility. Take the words of the witness in their entirety and see if they stand up to scrutiny. Most Pepie sightings that could be explained away by a mundane source are often cited as much by the witness. Other times, the witness may even share their own train of logic, often times stating that at first they thought it was "a log, an otter, a fish, etc." until it "rose up out of the water" in such a way that it no longer fit that possibility. The African tiger fish and the catfish of France are both known to leave the water to capture prey. The African tiger fish has been caught on film catching birds in midflight, whereas the catfish in certain French regions beach themselves to grab nearby pigeons. Of course the tiger fish would not survive the cold waters that one single winter would bring in Lake Pepin. Though never confirmed, people often claim observing species of bass and pike making similar mid-air prey catches. The adaptive behavior of the catfish leaving the water to capture prey has not been confirmed along the Mississippi River.

Of course, all of this only takes into account known species or natural phenomena. Needless to say, there are those that would speculate that the creature behind the Pepie sightings is prehistoric in origins and incorrectly thought to be extinct. Wherever you fall on this train of logic, there is some precedence for such theories. With this line of reasoning, we have quickly moved away from misidentification to witnessing something simply not known to science.

Any investigator of unexplained and mysterious events should remain vigilant to rule out any known phenomena or sources that could explain away the mystery. Once you take the step away from objective reasoning, you enter into the dark and twisty world of blind faith often ruled by emotion. Setting out to substantiate one's belief system is done at the expense of truth and at the peril of your own knowledge.

Chapter Eleven

Psychological Suggestion: A Willingness to Believe
by Chad Lewis

The truth behind the sightings becomes even murkier when the idea of suggestibility is thrown into the mix. The basic idea of suggestibility states that once a belief or idea permeates into an individual or community, that idea is more likely to play out than if the idea was never introduced. For example, once people heard of a serpent sighting in Lake Pepin, they would be more likely to attribute strange looking sightings of lateral waves, submerged logs and other aquatic animals to being that of a genuine sea serpent. This reasoning believes that newspapers that printed the original sightings inadvertently placed the suggestion in minds of others on the lake who would then conclude that they too had seen the serpent, rather than looking at other, more plausible causes for their sighting.

One problem with the idea of suggestibility arises in the fact that the people around Lake Pepin were pretty familiar with the 'normal' fish that inhabited their lake. In 1850, the *Burlington Hawk Eye* declared that Lake Pepin "abounds in Sturgeon," and in 1860, the *Pepin County Press* ran an article detailing the enormous size of the various fish in the lake, stating that pike, bass, cat-fish and sturgeon grow "to an almost incredible size" and are "easily captured" throughout the lake. In 1927, the *Alton Evening Telegraph* published a story about a gigantic alligator gar roaming the Mississippi River that was said to be over nine-foot long with 16-inch jaws. The 250 pound behemoth was "covered with heavy amour of bony scales" and was thought responsible for tearing other large fish in half.

Theories

> **Believed 9 Feet Long, with 16-Inch Jaws, Thought to Weigh at Least 250 Pounds.**

The Mississippi River is home to many large fish

This idea of suggestibility, when it comes to the paranormal is nothing new; for years scientists have been blaming the rising belief in the paranormal on media influence. With the amazing popularity of paranormal themed television shows like *Ghost Hunters, Monster Quest* and *Destination Truth*, along with nearly every horror movie released by Hollywood, interest in paranormal topics has never been higher.

In a 1985 article for *Skeptical Inquirer*, Paul Kurtz wrote that scientists believe that the media allows people to accept paranormal claims by promoting excessive attention to reports of paranormal experiences and by their unrelenting uncritical acceptance of the validity of these claims. This assumption that the media is influencing public beliefs was also supported by a 1981 study covered in James Alcock's book, *Parapsychology: Science or Magic?* Researchers found that respondents often cited stories from the media as their main reason for believing in the paranormal. Yet, not all studies implicate the media for our belief and subsequent sightings of paranormal activity. In 1997, the *Journal of Broadcasting & Electronic Media* contained the study "The Relationship Between Exposure to Televised Messages About Paranormal Phenomena and Paranormal Beliefs" which found that when the total number of hours watching television was used as an independent variable, no correlations emerged between viewing hours and beliefs in the paranormal. My own 2002 Master's Thesis (which was designed to investigate students' beliefs in the paranormal and to investigate the relationship between personal experience with a phenomenon, age, gender, interest in paranormal phenomena, spirituality and students' beliefs) found that students listed television as their number one source for gathering their information on the paranormal. Television as the source of information was closely followed by movies, friends, and books. Are we susceptible to media influence? The more intriguing question is this: how deep can that influence run? The problem with blaming all paranormal beliefs on media influence is that people believed in, and experienced, paranormal events long before newspapers, TV and radio... and certainly before Mulder and Scully were out chasing X-Files.

Photo courtesy of the Lake City Historical Society
Were the people of Lake Pepin susceptible to suggestion?

The idea of suggestibility also raises this poignant question: does seeing equal believing or does believing equal seeing? If someone goes to an alleged supernatural or paranormal location with the belief that something is going to happen, does that preconceived belief make it more likely that something will indeed happen? I dug a bit deeper into this question as part of my thesis, and what I discovered was a mixed bag of results. Those with a higher interest in paranormal phenomena were significantly more likely to have a personal experience with some paranormal phenomena (Ghosts & ESP) yet not for other phenomena (UFO, Bigfoot, and others). When specifically asked about hoaxes, I found that a high interest level in the paranormal was negatively correlated with the belief that others who report paranormal experiences with ghosts and the Loch Ness Monster are intentionally deceived or tricked by others. This means that those who have an interest in the Loch Ness monster DO NOT think that those who spot it are being tricked by hoaxers. Even more telling was that those with

Theories

a high interest in the paranormal were statistically more likely to believe that those who encountered the Loch Ness Monster were making contact with some level of awareness not yet understood by science.

As with most areas of the paranormal, we cannot completely rule out or dismiss the possibility of people becoming susceptible to suggestion with the legend of Pepie and that susceptibility influences their perception of events. However, the reverse of this could also be purposed by stating that because of the notoriety of Pepie, people near the lake have become more vigilant in looking for anything out of the ordinary, therefore more sightings take place. Unfortunately, the question of suggestibility cannot be fully discounted. Will there be cases where overzealous witnesses mistakenly see a floating log and believe it to be Pepie? Of course. At the same time, for every mistaken log or duck, there will be those sightings where the witness clearly spots a 12-foot neck popping out the water. I think that we all accept suggestibility as a real and potential explanation for some of the more mundane sightings, but these relatively few cases tend to be the exception, not the rule.

Chapter Twelve

Is Pepie a Hoax
by Chad Lewis

Skeptics will try to build a case that the sea serpent of Lake Pepin is nothing more than a hoax perpetrated by unknown publicity-seeking individuals. This idea does hold some credibility when placed next to the plethora of infamous hoaxes that are littered throughout the history of cryptozoology. In the eye of the general public, documented hoaxes like the Cardiff Giant, the Hodag, the Alien Autopsy film and the Fiji Mermaid share the same stage with nearly every other paranormal claim.

However, the main difference here is that most of the above mentioned hoaxes have all been single events and do constitute an overriding legend that has been in existence for hundreds of years. It may be easy to disprove one staged photo of a lake monster or Bigfoot; it is an entirely different challenge to dismiss the totality of hundreds of events surrounding each creature.

A Drawing of the infamous Fiji Mermaid

Theories

To fully analyze the evidence of Pepie as a hoax, we must start at the beginning. It is certainly possible that the local Native Americans created the serpent to easily fit into their known spiritual beliefs and rituals. Native lore is full of tales of giant serpents (Wakunja) that ruled the waters. Yet, this would place the creature more squarely into the category of Native folklore rather than an outright hoax. In this case, the creation of a specific serpent would be centered entirely to fulfill their spiritual beliefs rather than as a deliberate ruse. The main purpose of this type of serpent lore would be to serve as a cautionary tale about the dangers and hazards of the water and to keep their young from wandering off on their own. The problem lies in our inability to either prove or disprove this piece of Native lore. We may never know whether the Native people created the Lake Pepin creature out of pure imagination or if it was based on firsthand sightings. Regardless of the origin, the Native people feared the lake dwelling monster just the same.

It would also be a disservice not to look at the early newspaper accounts with some healthy skepticism. Having written several books on strange and bizarre newspaper stories from the late 1800s and early 1900s, I have encountered numerous stories that seem to bend credulity to the fullest. Newspapers of the late 1800s were filled with headlines that were given preference for their ability to sell copies, not for adhering to strict professional guidelines of integrity. However, I feel that many newspapers sported headlines that displayed their lack of knowledge and science more than an outright willingness to create fantastical stories. It is much easier today to look at the 1891 *Dallas Morning News* headline "Half Human, Half Monkey" and see that it was probably just a newborn suffering from Hypertrichosis. While a 1903 *Eau Claire Weekly Telegram* headline reported a woman's demise as "Cold Bath Causes Death" it is much more likely that the woman suffered a heart attack or brain aneurism while taking a bath. The majority of these wonderful headlines were the result of how primitive science and medicine were at the time, rather than an outward attempt to deceive.

Speaking specifically on sea serpent newspaper stories, it wasn't uncommon for resort towns to play up and embellish these sightings while talking with newspapers in hopes that a more sensational story would attract droves of tourists to their town. Yet, contrary to many other national serpent hot spots of the time, the towns around Lake Pepin seemingly made no attempt to capitalize on their amazing sightings (until just recently).

When discussing the trustworthiness of the newspaper accounts one must also consider the credibility of the witnesses. While some articles on serpent sightings were generic and nonspecific, the majority of them provided great detail as to who actually did the witnessing. Back in a time when communities were so close-knit, the good standing of a person's reputation played an enormous role in their ultimate success or failure. Some people may not have felt comfortable investing their life savings with a banker who had reported seeing serpents, or getting surgery from a doctor who spotted a monster in the water. As it turns out, the vast majority of sea serpent witnesses throughout the country were described as truthful upstanding citizens and pillars of the community. The probability that they would risk their good name and standing in the community in the pursuit of a serpent hoax seems rather unlikely, though not entirely unheard of. This is not to say that witnesses were infallible…on the contrary, many witnesses gave widely varying descriptions of the creatures they spotted. The early reports of the Lake Pepin beast range from it being a giant snake-like serpent with a long round body to that of some gigantic creature the size of an elephant which could move through the water with great rapidity. If mistakes in identification were made, it seems that misidentification would serve as more of the culprit than purposeful deception.

Of course, modern day witnesses are not bound by the same social pressures and morals that once kept people's honesty in check. One only needs to go online to find an overabundance of outright elaborate paranormal hoaxes—hoaxes that only seem to grow each day. When we take an in-depth look at the legend of Lake Pepin, we find several dubious photos, which are most likely hoaxes, even if no one has come forward to claim responsibly. Inevitability new hoaxes will arise—it is just part of the fabric of today's society—but they should have no bearing as to the integrity of
past sightings.

After poring over all the historical records, interviewing witnesses and completing two expeditions to Lake Pepin, I have reached the conclusion that although a hoax can never be completely ruled out, it holds little probability when assessing the origins of the Pepie legend.

Chapter Thirteen

Cryptozoological Potentials
by Noah Voss

With Pepie, we have an entire nation of pre-European people who believed of such a creature. In addition to that, we have dozens of documented sightings, including some with photographic data of something. This long history can be looked at several ways. First, one could argue that the original beliefs held by pre-pioneers would become the catalysts for newcomers to have those projected experiences. That view, of course, requires one to completely discount generations of entire nations of people's experiences to be entirely baseless. The other stance that is often taken as a result of these multigenerational experiences is that there sincerely is something mysterious being sighted that remains to be fully understood. If we follow this position, and further assume that the witnesses have not been misidentifying something known, the casualty of a hoax or the victim of their own mind, then, what else could Pepie possibly be?

The National Science Foundation has a project focusing, in part, on flora and fauna population estimates. Their "Tree of Life" project estimates that of the 1.7 million identified and known species on the planet Earth, there may be as many as 100 million total. Add to that the sobering statistic from the United Nations Environment Programme's estimate that 73,000 species become extinct annually. One might additionally consider the National Oceanic and Atmospheric Administration's (NOAA) estimate that 95% of the world's oceans remain unexplored and unseen by human eyes. Now, all of these big numbers and interesting percentages don't prove anything specifically, but I do feel that it begins to show the situation in an objective scientific light. It reveals a huge possibility, if not probability, in a quantitative perspective that there are species of large size that remain yet to be identified. The narrower question, and far more difficult one to answer, is if there is one of these unidentified species currently living in Lake Pepin. I further feel that this illumination of a fringe topic, easily pushed aside by detractors using low brow emotion, reveals the very real issue; that it is one very worthy of further research and investigation by scientists. Moreover, including the observational experiences of witnesses (that can either be verified by other data or add new data sets to the pool of information on the subject) will undoubtedly aid in revealing long term answers. What those answers are, as of yet, is open to much speculation.

Revisiting all these large numbers of possible global populations of unidentified species in another way should be enough to give the most ardent skeptic pause. After all, is there not an objective case to be made if there are upwards of 98 million species yet to be identified on the planet and 95% of the world's unexplored oceans for them to currently call home? Scientists, by definition, should take at least a passing interest in such 'monstrous' Pepie reports?

Is there precedence for such established western beliefs to be proven false?

Take the coelacanth for the classic, if not overused, example. It is a fish that was thought to have lived during the Paleozoic Era, or more specifically, the Devonian Period. This era would date it to have existed approximately 165 million years ago according to fossilized remains. It is estimated from currently available data that Coelacanthopsis evolved approximately 400 million years ago; the Coelacanth is its most recent in-

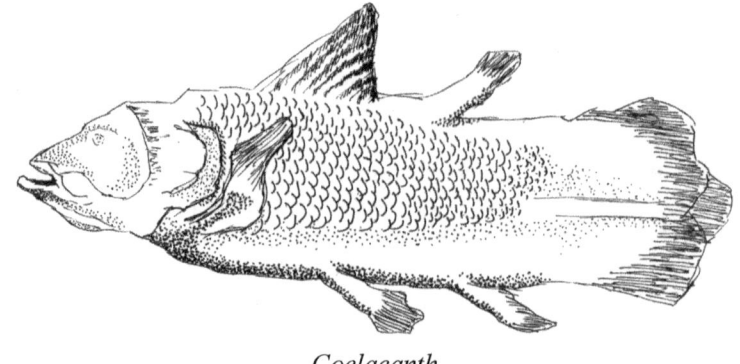

Coelacanth

Theories

carnation. Its fossilized remains were discovered and first named in 1839 and was globally recognized by experts to have gone extinct during the Cretaceous Period some 65 million years ago. To recap, a creature that can likely trace its evolutionary ancestry back 400 million years was thought to be extinct for 65 million years. That was, of course, until 1938.

It was then that a curator of a small museum was visiting a friend, who happened to be a ship's captain, and on her way to wish him a happy birthday, she just happened to notice an unusual fin protruding from his net full of the day's catch. Upon further investigation, she discovered the first known coelacanth semi-living specimen. I find it thought-provoking that before 1938, there had not even been any documented sightings of this fish; only fossilized remains. The Coelacanth can grow to six and a half feet long and almost 200 pounds. They seem to prefer the deep water, found around 2,300 feet under the ocean's surface, which may have helped significantly in remaining missed by modern eyes. The fact remains that this real world example illuminates the possibility, no matter how potentially slim, for setting precedence that Pepie may be something not yet recognized by modern science. If this would someday turn out to become a documented truth, then what could we speculate Pepie to be?

Long-necked plesiosaurus

Most cryptozoologists who study lake monster and sea serpent sightings are quick to place a plesiosaur species at the top of their suspect list. While I will agree that the long-necked plesiosaur fit some data nicely, I remain more dubious as a source for Pepie and most lake monsters in general. As we just discussed with the coelacanth, the fact that the plesiosaur is believed to have gone extinct approximately 65 million years ago may not be enough to completely remove it from the possible source for modern lake monster sightings. I do feel that it's not a great contender, however, because they lacked gills. This means, as a lung-based animal, they breathed air, which implies they would need to spend much time at the surface of the water over the course of their life. Even if they were able and preferred to stay submerged when they grabbed a breath of fresh air, like our modern turtles, this fact still would make me believe that more sightings of these creatures would exist. The estimated size of their brains also makes me lean towards not being overly sentient, such as dolphins could be. In addition, the position of the long-necked plesiosaur eyes would have very likely forced them to attack their prey from below. This speculated trait would again give them more reasons to be sighted more often on the surface than most lake monsters currently are due to their, at least occasional, surface feeding. However, it is only fair to say this information is all based off of limited knowledge gleamed from 65 million year old fossil remains. As we've observed, much can but often does not change in 65 million years. In my mind, there remains one clear fact when beginning down this path for possible sources for Pepie – the overwhelming number of possible options to choose from. If we decide to entertain the logic that something we thought was extinct may not be, then the options are limitless. The prehistoric choices become too many without more data to follow towards a narrowed candidate for the dinosaur or technically aquatic reptile version of Pepie.

Often times, the beluga whale or seal are cited as possible sources for lake monster sightings. In the case of Lake Pepin area sightings, the beluga whale doesn't fit due to the distinct white coloration of the mature whale and it's need to surface often in order to breath. Regarding the seal or pinniped species and this cryptozoological section of discussion, there is some merit to explore. While seals are obviously known to science around the world, there has been some debate over the purported long-necked seal. Its existence was first published in 1681 after Nehemiah Grew documented his encounter.

> PART I. *Of Fishes.*
>
> The LONG-NECK'D SEAL. I find him no where distinctly mention'd. He is much slenderer than either of the former. But that wherein he principally differs, is the length of his Neck. For from his Nose-end to his fore-Feet, and from thence to his Tail, are the same measure. As also in that instead of fore-Feet, he hath rather Finns; not having any Claws thereon, as have the other kinds.
>
> The SKULL of a SEAL. Given by *Henry Whistler* Esq;. The Teeth are shaped somewhat like a *Dogs*. The tops of them all are flat, being doubtless filed off. The *processus* of the *Os Frontis* which makes up the Orbit of the Eye in Land-Animals, is here wanting; and the said Bone pinched up much more narrowly: Both to make room, as it should seem, for a very large Eye. The passage into the Ears stands very oddly. In *Dogs, Cats*, and most other Land-Animals, forward and outwardly. But here it stands just oppositely, *sc.* behind and inwardly.
>
> The FORE-FOOT of a very great SEAL.

Image Credit: Nehemiah Grew's Musaeum Regalis Societatis—1681
Long-necked seal excerpt

In short, he documented that the length of this specimen was as long, from its snout to its forefeet, as it was from its forefeet to its tail – an increase in neck length of around 40% over other seal species. As one can imagine, this has been called into question by various skeptics and debunkers stating that Grew was confused. The normal posits are that Grew was duped by an exaggerated taxidermy specimen or that he was somehow unfamiliar with the serpentine structure of a seal's neck in a normal state. This classic "S" shaped neck form on a seal is held this way much the same as a turtle would pull its head into its own shell. While possible, these counterpoints seem thin when Grew's work as an accomplished observer, including his famous moniker given to him for his anatomy and physiology work as the "father of plant anatomy", are considered. In 2002, new fossilized findings out of Chili eventually led to a new species of extinct seal named Acrophocalongirostris. This seal has been dubbed by some as the 'swan-necked seal', however, the increase in neck length is noticeable;

it is only 4% longer than the neck of a current living seal. This is still a far cry from a plesiosaur.

In more recent times, Bernard Heuvelmans, known as the father of cryptozoology, proposed a new species to explain the overwhelming number of lake monster and sea serpent sightings. The name he gave this creature was Megalotarialongicollis and it looked decidedly crossed between a long-necked seal and plesiosaur or very near many of the monstrous sightings being witnessed around the globe. Until more quantifiable data surfaces to support this species projection, it too seems wanting as the source for Pepie.

The problem with a lung-filled, air breathing Pepie continues to bring me hesitation. Even if Pepie is a seal related species that can hold its breath for more than an hour as some can, it would still beg the question as to why there are not more sightings. Perhaps there are and these sightings are just not reported, or not reported to those with ties to a cryptozoologist, so they go undocumented. If we further examine Pepie as a seal related species or other semi-known species, we must also consider not just breeding populations but also why we have the severe lack of on land sightings. Of course, if we are contemplating a new species for the source of Pepie sightings, then we should also consider that it may have a unique breathing capability. The catfish, for example, can live for extended periods by breathing air or oxygen pulled in from their gills.

Scientists speculate the number of species ever to have lived on the planet Earth may number into the billions. This number is obviously an estimate, and more than complicated to actually predict. This current high-end estimate also includes much smaller species of life that would not be mistaken as Pepie the lake monster. These estimates show that there are nearly too many options to properly speculate though. By utilizing new data, including witness testimony, perhaps a smaller more manageable theory can be produced. For now, we are forced to wait for that data to find us, and on the extraordinary occasion, actively seek out.

Chapter Fourteen

UFO and Alien Connections
by Noah Voss

What do UFOs have to do with lake monsters? This is a fair question and one we will explore in some depth over the next chapter. There are two points that should be made upfront. First, as of now, there are no clear and direct connections to Pepie sightings and UFOs. The second point, however, clearly establishes that there is more than enough data surrounding and possibly connecting these two mysteries when it is examined on a global level. When surveying these documented UFO sightings, it is revealed that indeed something more complex is occurring contiguous to the UFO enigma as it may pertain to water and even cryptozoological creatures.

Let's break this up into more approachable sections, starting with Lake Pepin area UFO sightings.

The night of June 15, 1983, two witnesses driving on the back roads near Red Wing, Minnesota, watched an "unusually bright light" not more than 1,000 feet up in the air.

Not far from the northern end of Lake Pepin they gave chase in their car. The pair watched as the light became clearer, and a "definite triangular shape" was visible. The shape was uniquely "angled inwards at the back." The two continued following the UFO in their car at speeds nearing 90 mph. Within seconds they reported that it sped off into the northwest until out of view.

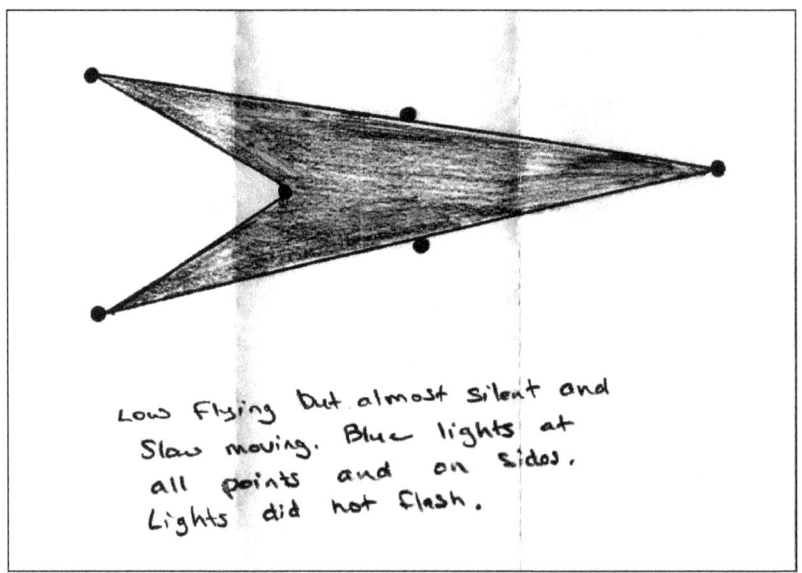

A sketch made by Sean Bindley documenting his July 2004 Long Lake UFO sighting

On May 15, 2013, a triangle UFO was again reported with "three orange lights" moving east across the skies above Red Wing, Minnesota, and the northern end of Lake Pepin.

Our next UFO report comes from Frontenac, Minnesota, on the western shores of Lake Pepin. The husband and wife witnesses were camping and enjoying some early spring star gazing in March of 2001. They noticed a "soundless fast moving craft" that had a "pulsating" red light on the bottom. The witness stated that he grew up very near an air force base as the son of an aeronautics engineer and felt very comfortable identifying many aircraft, day or night. In his own words, this craft was different. The UFO moved from south to north, running parallel with Lake Pepin until out of view.

Moving further south to Alma, Wisconsin, puts our next strange UFO sighting just past the southernmost end of Lake Pepin and on the shores of the Mississippi River. It was November 2011 when a 51-year-old hunter was enjoying spotting satellites sputter across the dark sky before the opening morning of deer hunting. Excited to see two shooting stars already this morning, our witness watched what he initially thought was another satellite until it came to a dead stop in the sky. This in itself could be quite unusual; however what he reported next is a regular occurrence in many UFO sightings—it began to zigzag. The UFO made a "series of 45 degree turns" with sharp changes in direction each time. He continued to watch the UFO repeat this similar maneuver for many minutes until the sun rose. Though the sky lightened, our witness reported that this UFO was one of the last lights left to be seen as the day became brighter. Thankfully observant qualities run in his family; later in the day his 20-year-old nephew, who was also hunting in nearby woods, reported seeing the same UFO perform the same strange movements.

If we move just a few miles northeast of Lake Pepin, there are countless UFO reports from the area of Elmwood, Wisconsin. The wave of UFO sightings in the1970s in that area made news around the world—nearly culminating into the world's first UFO landing port. Indeed, in my 2008 book *UFO Wisconsin: A Progress Report* I detail dozens of these UFO sightings, as Elmwood made the top 5 UFO hotspot list. One startling UFO sighting from the area includes Police Officer George Wheeler's up-close sighting of a large silver craft hovering low over the local rock quarry.

That sighting ended for Officer Wheeler when he reported that a blue light shot from the craft, striking him as he sat in the driver's seat of his patrol car. That is where he was found moments later, unconscious, by the local police chief. Perhaps stranger still, Officer Wheeler's patrol car wouldn't start and later needed to be towed, despite having all routine maintenance records. The UFO had fled the scene, but the sighting was corroborated by more than a dozen other witnesses who saw it as it left the area. Officer Wheeler passed away within a year of this UFO encounter.

Clearly there are UFO sightings from the Lake Pepin area that range from a few mysterious lights and unexplained crafts to those that are downright terrifying encounters with Unidentified Flying Objects. More to the investigation of Pepie the lake monster, we must ask if there are connections between UFOs and water specifically that would allow us to follow some data trail to potential connections.

Unidentified Flying Objects or UFOs have a long and debated history. Unidentified Submerged Objects or USOs also have a very long history, however a much less discussed one.

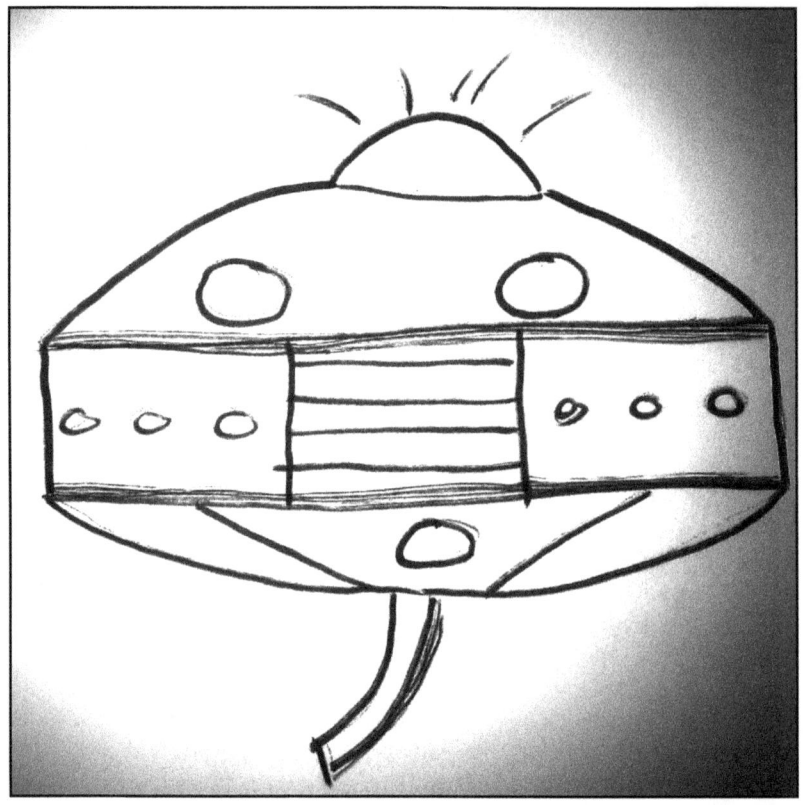

Sketch provided by UFOwisconsin.com
UFO image based on Officer George Wheeler's own drawings made from his April 22, 1976 sighting

Simply put, USOs are unidentifiable objects witnessed beneath any body of water's surface. These USO sightings basically fall into three categories. First those objects that never break the surface plane of the water and through the entire sighting remain submerged. A second type is witnessed initially as a classic flying UFO only to submerge at some point during the sighting. The third and final categorization for our needs is reported by experiencers who witness an unidentified submerged object and watch as it lifts from the water and becomes a classic flying UFO sighting. What we're missing here is the obvious connection between lake monsters and UFOs or even USOs. There are still precedents set that should solicit dis-

Theories

cussion of connected possibilities, even if USO sightings from the Lake Pepin area have yet to reach me. We can look to the Eastern Canadian coastal village of Shag Harbor to bring a real life UFO turned USO event. It was in October 1967 that Royal Canadian Mounted Police (RCMP) Ron Pound watched as a strangely lit object moved across the night sky. Constable Pound initially thought he was watched a plane about to crash into the harbor. At least 11 other witnesses independently watching this same event unfold, many of them terrified that they, too, were witnessing a plane about to crash. Those in the nearby town who didn't witness the UFO reported strange noises at the time the UFO was crashing through the sky. Stranger still, many of the witnesses didn't report that the UFO crashed into the water; rather it stopped short of the water's surface. The UFO was reported to have hovered there for some time. Eventually the UFO entered the water, and witnesses described at that point there remained "glittery" yellow "oily" foam on the surface of the water, nearly 80 feet wide. A light, glowing from beneath the surface of the water was reported by the earliest witnesses, and the strange yellow foam was later substantiated by the rescue Coast Guard Cutter. It was all hands on deck as the police and civilians rushed to the area of the crash, hoping to find survivors—or at least more clues to the mystery. Nothing was found but the unexplained yellow foam. Divers from the Royal Canadian Navy even searched the cold water over the following days, expecting to find some wreckage. The search continued but no planes with flight plans through the area were reported missing, and no debris was ever allegedly found. Despite the Canadian Navy and Coast Guard's documented involvement, the story fizzled out of the news and may have been dismissed forever as a misidentified meteorite or Soviet Union space project.

That is, until 1993—when the Mutual Unidentified Flying Object Network (MUFON) investigators dug further. What they turned up was an amazing additional tale to the public reports of the 1967 Shag Harbor incident. Their investigation discovered many more witnesses than were initially interviewed by the press in 1967. These latest witnesses were able to add much to what happened after the UFO submerged into the water. It seems that a submarine detection base discovered the USO on its monitoring equipment. MUFON investigators Chris Styles and Doug Ledger continued to have supportive witnesses that unfortunately would not officially go on the record due to worries of losing jobs, family, friends and pensions, while only finding jail time. These anonymous witnesses reported that salvage operations were being made when a second USO joined the first. Those involved in this watch and wait were called away to investigate an incursion of a reported Soviet submarine further north. As the Navy vessels left the area, the two USOs reportedly began moving again, remaining under water the entire time until clear of all witnesses. It is assumed that at that point they lifted to the water's surface and shot off into the sky. Indeed, UFOlogists have pieced together radar returns of UFOs sighted just to the north of Shag Harbor by the ship M.V. Dickerson with eighteen hands, as well as sightings from Air Canada Flight 305 where the pilot and co-pilot both filed official reports just hours before the Shag Harbor incident. It seems that there was much about this case that the general media missed on the first go-around.

Another USO incident worth mentioning happened not far from the Pascagoula River in Mississippi. It was 1973 when eight fishermen aboard their boat chased a USO not far under the water's surface. This object was illuminated until the fisherman drew close, and they even attempted to probe at the object with their long oars. Each time the light would extinguish as it moved away. The atmosphere only became more stressful for the fisherman as the sighting drew on. Normally netting 2,000 pounds worth of catch, this night they found no more than 400 pounds—and those nets nearest the object came up empty. They eventually made their way to the area coast guard to report their experience. After much hesitation, the coastguard dispatched Lawrence Nations and Charles Crews. Their official report shows they had the same USO experience, describing a matching scenario to the fisherman's. A search was performed the following day by the Coast Guard, though yielding nothing. Their reports drew the attention of the Naval Ship Research and Development Laboratory in Florida, who sent investigators to interview witnesses. Perhaps this USO was nothing more than a yet-to-be-discovered sea creature making its first appearance to human eyes.

What makes this otherwise unusual case even more noteworthy is the report that came only a few weeks prior to this one and only a bit closer to shore in the mouth of the Pascagoula River. Two friends and coworkers, Charles Hickson and Calvin Parker, had finished up work and planned to spend the rest of the evening fishing in the shipyard of the Pascagoula River. What unfolded soon after that began with a bright light and a strange noise causing them to turn around. Behind them hovered an oblong craft about a foot above the ground and approximately 100 feet in length. A door somehow appeared on the side and out came three semi-human creatures. Calvin and Charles were frozen—unable to move—as these three entities floated without moving their legs, took hold of them, and floated them onboard their craft.

Theories

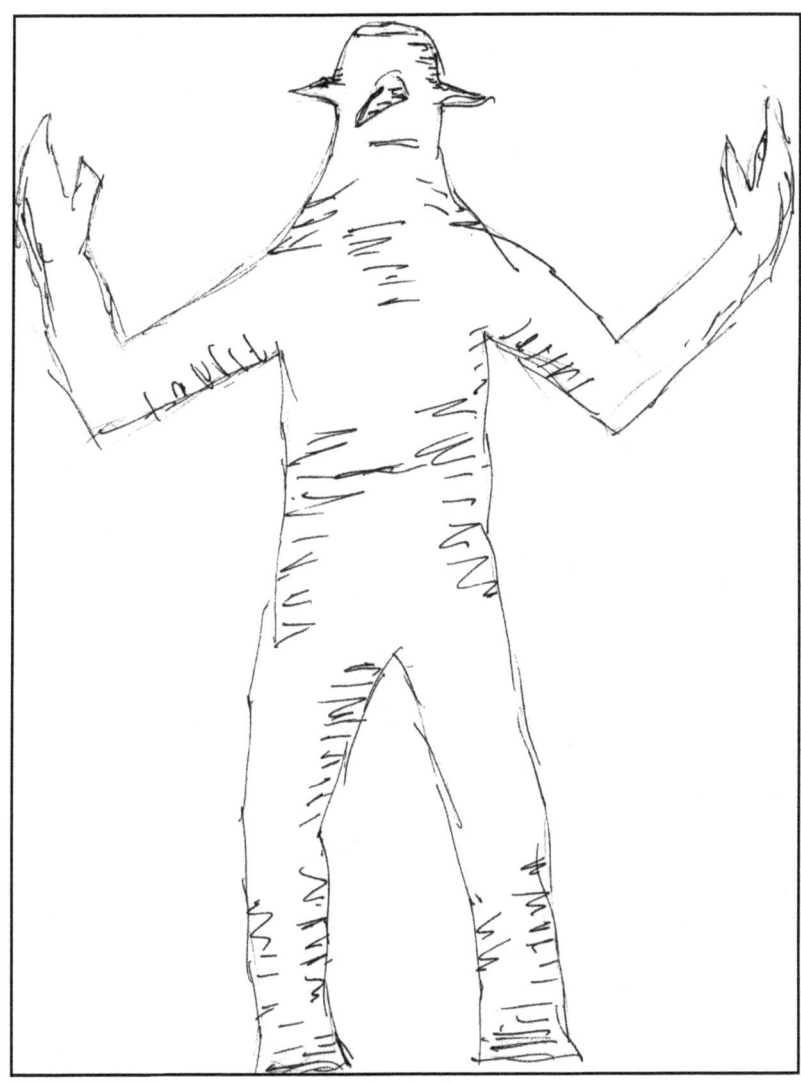

Alien from Pascagoula abduction as described by co-workers Charles Hickson and Calvin Parker

Perhaps 30 minutes of examinations were conducted inside the UFO. The next moment they can recall, they were standing back on the shore facing the water. Terror stricken, the two sat in their car for nearly 45 minutes trying to figure out what had just transpired and what to do next. This would go on to be a heavily scrutinized UFO abduction case. UFOlogists descended on the area and were able to document independent witnesses that corroborated portions of their experience. Charles passed away in 2011, his story never changed. Calvin's recounting of the UFO abduction events has not wavered. Though it may be nothing more than coincidence, it remains interesting enough to note the Pascagoula River opens into the Gulf of Mexico, not far from the Mississippi River delta.

These reports of UFOs diving into or launching out of bodies of water and abductions by strange entities are documented around the globe by private citizens, public company employees and government agencies. Still, regarding Lake Pepin, a direct link to someone witnessing a creature matching Pepie around the same time as a UFO (or, even better, a USO) it has just not been documented. We are left to only speculate and discuss historic cases that may have parallels, should the data to connect them ever emerge. So, if not lake monsters, then how about UFO sightings in the area of chupacabra-looking creatures? Or maybe metallic robotic-like droids exiting UFOs? Why not bigfoot leaving landed UFOs or even piloting them? Indeed, all of these scenarios have each been documented.

In 1969, author Warren Smith documented an extraordinary bigfoot case in *Strange Monsters and Madmen*. It seems that James C. Wyatt's grandfather kept a journal of his pioneer travels. He had documented his own experience during his overwintering with an Indian tribe. During this stay, he was taken to visit a being that the Indians called "crazy bear," and he soon found out the hairy creature was covered in shiny black hair except where the skin shown through around the eyes and palms on each hand. The journal reportedly goes on to explain that the crazy bears were sky people, many of whom who had been left in a nearby valley. They were placed there by "small moons" that had hairless humans who wore shiny clothes. Warren Smith has since passed, however his source for this legend was Brad Steiger. Mr. Steiger had received copied pages of Wyatt's journal. The whole story sounds like a space ship landed full of humans wearing spacesuits, dropping off bigfoot creatures. Unfortunately, it is very difficult to verify the authenticity of these historical cases, though we do have additional oral traditions from other peoples recounting very similar stories. Of course, we don't have to look any further from Lake Pepin than in its bordering state of Wisconsin.

Theories

I interviewed author Jack Kewaunee Lapseritis in 2007 for a UFO case I was working on at that time. Mr. Lapseritis had already been studying many mysteries for several years at that point, and his book *The Psychic Sasquatch* detailed several UFO bigfoot connections right from Wisconsin. After one well-known UFO sighting in the state, his interviews revealed that multiple witnesses in two cars watched as a UFO lifted from the ground. The UFO disappeared into the sky, leaving behind a giant creature described as a large, hairy bigfoot that quickly disappeared into the nearby woods.

During December 1974, near Frederic, Wisconsin, local farmer William Bosak was returning home in the dark of night. As fog began to cover the road, he was forced to a stop by a large UFO in his path. As William drove around it, he reported clearly seeing a large hairy ape-like creature inside. The UFO rose into the air and disappeared.

Perhaps stranger still, we could look to the famed Skinwalker Ranch in Utah. There the UFO sightings go from strange to beyond comprehension...though somewhere in the middle rest multiple witnesses who reported giant wolves appearing around strange lights in the night sky.

Ultraterrestrial sources for the odd sightings around the Skinwalker Ranch are often theorized, but what about Pepie? Ultraterrestrials are repeatedly speculated to be some form of life that is interacting with our own reality. Where ultraterrestrials may be coming from or going to is just as large of a debate as their conceivable existence. Those that hazard a theory have stated these beings may normally be in a different time, place or entirely other reality. This concept may have basis someday from the theoretical frameworks such as M-theory, string theory, multiverse theories and more coming from one of the greatest minds of our century—studying the field of quantum physics. Renowned researcher John A. Keel often speculated that the Mothman was perhaps an ultraterrestrial attempting to communicate with people in our reality. Sadly, there is currently no data to follow coming from Lake Pepin that would lead us to this conclusion, other than a series of strange and unexplained sightings around the area.

What we are still missing is the direct data set that would allow us to make a methodical, albeit exotic, connection between lake monsters and UFOs. We have, however, now begun the important discussion that goes beyond simple categorization of unexplained phenomena casually placed into tidy and clearly inappropriate groups. There are strange things being sighted in the waters of Lake Pepin and in the skies above. For now, we just don't know if there is any connection.

Chapter Fifteen

The $50,000 Reward For Pepie
by Chad Lewis

One aspect of the Pepie legend that sets it apart from nearly all other modern cryptozoological creatures is the addition of a $50,000 reward that has been offered to anyone who can provide conclusive proof of its existence. The idea for the reward originated one evening as Lake City, Minnesota, businessman Larry Nielson was watching a television program on the legend of Scotland's Loch Ness Monster. Nielson had recently discovered an 1871 newspaper report about some sort of water creature inhabiting Lake Pepin, and throughout the program Nielson noted the similarities between the legend of Loch Ness and that of Lake Pepin. The only real difference between the two was that the Loch Ness Monster was nearly universally recognized, while the legend of Pepie remained all but unknown. Believing that the town's unique history was being underutilized, Nielson decided that Pepie was in dire need of some promotion, and thus the idea for the $50,000 reward was born. When Nielson excitedly told his wife about his reward idea she asked, "what if someone actually captures the creature and gets the reward. You will be out $50,000!" Thinking of the scientific discoveries that would follow, along with the throngs of tourists that would flock to Lake Pepin if the creature was ever captured, Nielson replied, "it would be the best $50,000 I could ever spend!" With the reward offering Nielson was unknowingly following in the footsteps of the great showman, P.T. Barnum, who in 1873 famously offered $50,000 for the hide of the Lake Champlain Monster (Champ).

Nielson's unique plan for garnering publicity for Pepie worked—news of the reward attracted immense media attention from around the country. It was no surprise that the $50,000 reward was the main selling point, however, many of the TV, radio and newspaper reports also gave a fair amount of time to the history and legend of Pepie sightings.

Now before you grab your camera and fishing gear and venture off for Lake Pepin, it should be noted that it will take much more than a blurry photo or some grainy out-of-focus video in order for you to claim the reward. In fact, if you want to become $50,000 richer, you will need to bring forth undisputable proof in the form of a photo of the creature that can be authenticated and/or you can simply capture the beast—or at least a piece of it that can be analyzed to show it originated from some yet undiscovered species (or one thought to be extinct). One other caveat of the reward is that whether you are going to capture it in a net, catch it with a fishing pole, trap it in shallow water or just old fashioned wrestle it into submission, Pepie cannot be harmed in the process.

As of today, numerous eyewitness accounts of the mysterious serpent have been reported and several compelling photos of the alleged creature have been taken, yet no conclusive proof has surfaced—the reward is still up for grabs!

Photo courtesy of Larry Nielson www.pepie.net
One of the many spots around Lake Pepin to report your sighting

Theories 129

Searching for Pepie (L to R) John Sturdy - Director of Photography with the Sturdy Group, Chad Lewis, and Damen Shaqiri- Sound Engineer for Evolv Media.

Pepie: The Lake Monster of the Mississippi River

Final Thoughts

Chapter Sixteen

A Biased View of Objectivity
by Noah Voss

Investigating real-life mysteries, especially those that can at least touch on the paranormal, can have different nuances than writing on some pop culture trend and how much one loves or hates it. Not to belittle anyone else's passion, rather opinions matter most in those fashionable circles. The author's background often subjectively raises the editorialization to monstrously mythic proportions. When one's unscientifically formed opinion artificially carries such undeserving weight, many things can happen. For example, we need to look no further than televisions portrayal of the paranormal over the last decade or more. Passionate opinions of love or hate have little benefit to dispassionate answers sought during methodical adventures into dark and dangerous mysteries. Though perhaps an entertaining approach for some to read or others to watch, such enthusiastically confident parroting droned on as fact in the paranormal field, it remains that authors of such sentiments spout stances often indefensible if we disallow subjective emotional beliefs in any portion of their position. Here is where the balance must be struck for knowledge to be gained efficiently. Not ineffectively connecting two or more unrelated observations because it substantiates your predetermined belief system. Nor should we blindly dismiss first-hand eyewitness accounts of unexplained phenomena. Somewhere between these two commonly treaded paths in the paranormal lolls objectivity. After all, mysteries are by nature born of fractional views of a complete story. The obscured portions are my quarry. When I am seeking the masked remnants of the narrative, I take great aim to put the story together without preconceived notions of reality. I embrace the fact that whatever I discover may not be what my subconscious hopes to find. To purely allow the facts to lead my investigation's next step is the essence of an ideal case.

Final Thoughts

Through my roughly two decades adventuring around the world chasing mysteries, I haven't ever truly solidified any resolute convictions. Upon further self-reflection now, if I had any innate touch-stones, I suppose it would be objectivity.

It's easier for most to dismiss such fanciful mysteries, such as lake monsters, before ever reviewing any of the data surrounding it, rather than to even consider the possibility. Remaining skeptical seems like a healthy approach to most things in life, unexplained creature sightings included. It is far beyond skepticism to blindly reject the idea of Pepie.

Assimilating new world views with your old ones is not an easy task for everyone. This becomes more difficult for people to embrace when the new truths are unnerving due to their incompleteness. Is this not how we've watched knowledge spread through cultures over recorded history? The most popular question I receive when presenting on lake monsters such as Pepie is "do you believe it exists?" A fair question, though I always caution that the Pepie topic and lake monster idea on a whole is larger than any five second sound bite and sadly demanding of more than a one word answer. The closest I can come to succinctly answering is that it currently appears something out of the ordinary is happening at Lake Pepin.

To take the next logical progression then, I feel strongly that when something truly out of the ordinary occurs, it fully warrants more research and investigation. I remain hopeful that the exploration of mysteries continually leads to a greater and fuller understanding of simply everything around us. More research in this case could reveal a monstrous creature living in Lake Pepin or no lake monster at all. Further examination may just illuminate a new understanding of human psychology, but both potentials remain valid motivators for more investigation.

I do have some ideas that I would like to explore on my future expeditions to Lake Pepin. I would love to have better underwater audio recording equipment. This would allow us to capture or rule out any potential creature that may be moving through the water utilizing audible echo locating. I would love to be able to create a few additional underwater camera rigs for the obvious reasons of capturing more video footage from beneath the water's surface. Even just to have more time to put our investigative tools into longer use on Lake Pepin and preferably from a few more boats. By purchasing this book, visiting our websites, and following our videos you have helped to support us, and by doing so, have made it that much more feasible to dig further into mysteries like Pepie.

The unexplained remains so because the research is not whole. Witness experiences are often the final pieces added to a mystery that bring an entirety back to the picture.

Regularly in my research I end up including as much space to debunking the unexplained events as I do to supporting their paranormal potential. I hold great respect for people willing to calmly come forward and add constructively to the Pepie conversation on either side of the examination.

During my recent travels to Massachusetts Bay, home to perhaps the first sea serpent report in America, I noted in my research the common practice of removing validity from witnesses. Even when the witnesses are not selling anything or seeking anything other than sharing their observations, they seem to enrage their critics with some sort of perceived attack. If we look more closely at the first sea serpent sighting, we find John Josselyn. He was a well-to-do citizen from the 1600s who indulged his passions in medicine and botany. He seems to have observed the world around him, embraced the vastness, and attacked the unknown by documenting what he could. He was fortunate enough to be financially secure, and with his brother in colonial Main government, he additionally came from a well-respected family. This allowed him to approach his work without dire need of monetary reward—ahh the dream. Mr. Josselyn was praised for his publications in the 1670s. His *An Account of the Voyages to New England, London* was acclaimed as "the earliest on the natural history of the region" and "an extensive and quite accurate catalog of the fauna and flora of the region." His documentations in *New England's Rarities, discovered in Birds, Beasts, Fishes, Serpents, and Plants of that Country* was so well received it has critical editions of these works published as recently as 1988. The Wisconsin State Historical Society writes that he "provides us with the most complete natural history of New England during the early years of the English settlement, as well as acute observations on the impact of settlement on both Indian society and American flora and fauna." So how could someone who accomplished all this, and even influenced Henry David Thoreau's work, fall from graces and be outcast by critics to the level of attacking his frankness, style, and high level of gullibility touting his naiveté? Well, Mr. Josselyn included in his upstanding and accepted writings two fatal topics. The first was critical observations of the preva-

Final Thoughts

lent religion at the time. The second was eyewitness accounts of sea serpents sprinkled through his writing. I nearly fell victim to his detractor's narrow view of life, not once, but twice, as recently as 2007 and 2013. During those years, I found myself adventuring through the dark back roads of the Massachusetts area across the bay and into the Atlantic. As per norm, before any proper adventure, the research must be performed ad nauseam. With the dozens of mysteries I had dug up to explore on my travels through several states during both trips, I came across the sea serpent sightings as documented by Mr. Josselyn. Both times I relegated them to a lower level due to the perceived controversy surrounding him. It was only during the writing of this lake monster book that I was able to justify the countless hours needed to sort out the most objective viewpoint on their serpent mystery. In short, Mr. Josselyn seems to have quite objectively and clearly documented what was told to him by witnesses, taking no strong stance one way or the other as to his persuasion. His witnesses were comprised of the usual suspects. Ship captains who spent months at a time crossing the ocean also relied daily on their ability to harvest creatures from the water. Native peoples, who were not just close to the water as an essential part of their food supply, also spiritually observed the coming and goings the water brought for generations. Just as with Pepie, there were likely hundreds of years of sightings, probably at least one hoax, and more than one critic. The issue becomes, even with hindsight, the view of the serpent sightings is relegated to the detractor's simple and wildly inaccurate view that points only to the hoax and the ad hominem attacks on those giving voice to the witnesses. Sadly, those types of detractions can often be accomplished in half the words that an objective review of the supportive points can.

I don't believe myself to be so embittered that I grasp onto any thought that the masses don't, in some misguided attempt at creating my counter culture independent identity. I see real, tangible, and beneficial results coming out of solving mysteries such as Pepie. Perhaps someone reading this will discover the next piece to solve the mystery surrounding Pepie.

Remember, adventures come to the adventuresome.

Noah Voss

Chapter Seventeen

Long Live Pepie!
by Chad Lewis

Over the years, I have investigated the entire laundry list of various paranormal phenomena. Crop circles, UFOs, haunted places, cursed objects, out-of-body experiences, ESP, near-death experiences, portals to hell, alien abductions, and nearly anything else you can think of. Yet, out of all of these varied phenomena, chasing so-called "monsters" still ranks as my all-time favorite. In my quest to uncover these unknown beasts, I have tracked Vampire folklore through Transylvania, searched the jungles of Belize for the elusive Tata Duende, pursued El Chupacabras through Central America, and traipsed through numerous forests hot on the trail of Bigfoot. Yet, reigning supreme above all other creatures is my passionate interest in sea serpents. I blame my professional fascination with serpents on my home state of Wisconsin. Back in the late 1800s and early 1900s, Wisconsin was home to dozens of lake, rivers, and streams that were said to be inhabited by some sort of aquatic beast. So, it seems synchronistic that a WI/MN serpent would be at the heart on my latest adventure.

Anyone who spends enough time actively researching the paranormal finds that their views and theories often progress and shift, moved by the evidence (or lack thereof) from hundreds of cases. Burnout is common, disillusionment is frequent, and even the most ardent of researchers can find their interest dissolved by the utter inability to prove or disprove the very thing they are researching. Far too often, society wants to paint beliefs into a black or white issue. Do you believe in ghosts? Do you think Bigfoot is real? In actuality, I have discovered that many of the finest researchers

Final Thoughts

I work with have adopted a 50/50 stance when it comes to different phenomena. They believe there is a fifty percent chance that something could exist and fifty percent that it doesn't; simple, safe, and accurate. Without fail, I nearly always find myself squarely entrenched in this camp, unable to fully commit to one side or the other. I often state that after 20 some odd years of researching the weird and unusual, I am simply left with more questions than answers.

Chad Lewis on the hunt for Pepie

When I first began researching Pepie, I had no idea that this would be the rare case that would actually catapult me from the comforts of my 50/50 stance. It happened during the middle of our second expedition at Lake Pepin. Noah and I had just finished fixing our sonar equipment and were taking some time to slow down and bask in the beauty of the lake. As our boat slowly drifted downstream, I asked Noah what he thought the possibility was that Pepie was an undiscovered sea serpent. Noah is a seasoned researcher and an expert in the paranormal field, so it wasn't surprising that he gave it the traditional 50/50 assessment. Now, 99 out of a 100 times, I would have espoused the same exact 50/50 rationale, but much to my own surprise, when tasked with the same question, I blurted out "75 percent". Amazingly, Pepie had done what I would have deemed improbable;

it resurrected my belief in mystery again. Let me be clear, I love the adventure of the road, the excitement of the legend, the trials of digging up new research, and I unflinchingly cling to the hope that someday all of my research will point to something. Yet, years and years of the daily research grind had eroded my belief that something else existed outside of our own realm. There, situated in the middle of a lake on the Mississippi River, I was once again filled with wonder and awe at the growing possibility brewing in my mind that something unknown was truly lurking beneath the waters of Lake Pepin.

Of course, the million dollar question then becomes, "what is Pepie?" If in fact, we are dealing with a flesh and blood creature, then we know absolutely nothing about its life and habits. Based on the lack of any modern reports to the contrary, Larry Nielson told me he firmly believes that the creature is harmless, and quite possibly, even friendly like "dolphins and porpoises," sustaining itself on shad and other smaller fish. Others take a more sinister outlook, viewing it as a deadly force, using Lake Pepin as its hunting grounds. What it eats, if there is a breeding population, if it can maneuver on land, if there is more than one type, if it can migrate; the sheer number of unanswered questions is staggering. Perhaps the serpents that were once sighted throughout the Mississippi River have become trapped in Lake Pepin by the dozens of lock and dams which would have restricted the movement of any large creature. I think this book does an excellent job addressing many of the popular and obscure theories about Pepie, and maybe someday these questions will be definitely answered. Based on my extensive research and personal expeditions to Lake Pepin, I do believe that something living is responsible for the creation of the Pepie legend. For me, the accumulation of so many credible sightings has ruled out many of the explanations of Pepie being nothing more than a hoax, or misidentification of wakes, or half submerged logs. Whether Pepie is simply a huge sturgeon, gigantic catfish, or an entirely new undiscovered species, I can't say. But I firmly believe that something big and real has been the cause behind the sightings in Lake Pepin and the greater Mississippi River for hundreds of years. Regardless of what the future holds for Pepie, I can only hope that, much like it did for me, Pepie continues to inspire curiosity and mystery in all those who cross its path.

Keep an eye out!

Bibliography

Chapter 1. Unearthing a Legend
Janesville Gazette August 24, 1867.
Nielson, Larry. Personal Interview. July, 2011.

Chapter 2. Brief History of Lake Pepin: The Lake of Tears
Centralia Enterprise And Tribune 19 July, 1890.
Daily Gazette, July 15, 1890.
Lake City Historical Society. *Lake City, Minnesota Our Historical Journal.* Virginia Beach: The Donning Company Publishers, 2007.
Milwaukee Weekly Wisconsin 19 July, 1890

Chapter 3. The Tragic Tale of Maiden Rock
Arizona Independent Republic 30 June, 1940
Eastman, Mary. *Dahcota: or, Life and Legends of the Sioux Around Fort Snelling.* 1849.
Eau Claire News 12 June, 1886.
Pike, Zebulon Montgomery. *The expeditions of Zebulon Montgomery Pike:to headwaters of the Mississippi River, through Louisiana territory, and in New Spain, during the years 1805-6-7.* New York: F.P.Harper, 1895.
Wilder, Laura Ingalls. *A Homemaker of the Ozarks. Missouri Ruralist,* 1914.

Chapter 4. Native American Sightings and Folklore
Heuvelmans, Bernard. *In the Wake of Sea Serpents.* London: Rupert Hart-Davis Ltd. 1968.
Lake City Historical Society. *Lake City, Minnesota Our Historical Journal.* Virginia Beach: The Donning Company Publishers, 2007.
Lewis, Chad. *The Wisconsin Road Guide to Mysterious Creatures.* Eau Claire: On the Road Publications. 2011.

Chapter 5. Pioneer Sightings
Janesville Gazette 24 August, 1867.
Hennepin, Louis. *A New Discovery of a Vast Country in America.* 1600s.
Lake City Historical Society. *Lake City, Minnesota Our Historical Journal.* Virginia Beach: The Donning Company Publishers, 2007.
Pierce County Herald. 14 July, 1875
Semi-Weekly Wisconsin. 28 July, 1875.
Wabasha Daily Sentinel 26 April 1871.

Chapter 6. Modern Sightings
"Alien Bigfoot, Cajun Werewolf, Lake Pepin Monster." *Monsters and Mysteries in America*. Destination America. 14 April, 2014. Television.
Freier, Heidi. Telephone and Email Interview. April 2014.
Nielson, Larry. Personal Interview. September, 2013.
Raymond, Steve. Telephone and Email Interview. April, 2014
Scott, Tom. Telephone Interview. April, 2014
Stone, Chuck. Telephone Interview. April, 2014
Durand Courier-Wedge 3 December, 1987.
"The Monster of Lake Pepin." *Life to the Max*. WCCO-TV. 31 October, 2009. Television.

Chapter 9. Other Monsters Seen in the Mississippi River
Alton Evening Telegraph October 1, 1927
Altoona Mirror 24 November, 1919.
Anita Tribune 17 June, 1886.
Burlington Hawk Eye 27 June, 1850.
Burlington Hawk Eye 25 October, 1877.
Connersville Examiner 16 October, 1877.
Derrick, 28 September, 1877.
Indianapolis People 27 October, 1877.
Memphis Reveille 18 October, 1877.
Petersburg Index And Appeal 10 September, 1877.
Semi Weekly Iowa State Reporter 6 October, 1903.
Stevens Point Daily Journal 12 January, 1878.
Stevens Point Daily Journal 19 January. 1878

Chapter 10. Misidentifications
American Journeys. "John Josselyn." Accessed 2014. http://www.americanjourneys.org/aj-107/summary/index.asp
Coleman, L. and Huyghe, P. *The Field Guide to Lake Monsters, Sea Serpents, and Other Mystery Denizens of the Deep*. Tarcher/Penguin, New York. 2003.
Cucherousset J, Boulêtreau S, Azémar F, Compin A, Guillaume M, (2012) "Freshwater Killer Whales: Beaching Behavior of an Alien Fish to Hunt Land Birds," *PLoS ONE peer-reviewed, open access scientific journal*. e50840. doi:10.1371/journal.pone.0050840, December 2012
Forbes, Stephen Alfred, *The Fishes of Illinois*. Illinois Printing Company, Danville Illinois. 1908

G. C. O'Brian, F. Jacobs, S. W. Evans and N. J. Smit. January 2014 "First observation of African tigerfish Hydrocynus vittatus predating on barn swallows Hirundo rustica in flight," *Journal of Fish Biology.* Volume 84, Issue 1, Pages 263-266

Heuvelmans, B. *In the Wake of the Sea-Serpents.* Hill and Wang, 1968.

Josselyn, John. *Account of Two Voyages to New-England Made during the Years 1638, 1663.* Boston: William Veazie, 1865.

Josselyn, John *Colonial Traveler: A Critical Edition of Two Voyages to New-England.* 1988.

Nehemiah Grew, *Musaeum Regalis Societatis: Or a catalogue and description of the natural and artificial rarities.* 1681

Taylor, M.P., Wedel, M.J., and Naish, D. 2009. "Head and neck posture in sauropod dinosaurs inferred from extant animals," Acta Palaeontologica Polonica. 54 (2): 213–220. DOI:10.4202/app.2009.000

United States Geological Survey. "Seismic Seiches." Accessed 2014. http://earthquake.usgs.gov/learn/topics/seiche.php

Watermolen, D. J. and Murrell, M. D. "Checklists of Wisconsin Vertebrates," Wisconsin Department of Natural Resources. 2001

Chapter 11. Psychological Suggestion

Alcock, J. E. *Parapsychology: Science or magic?* Oxford, Pergamon Press. 1981.

Kurtz, P. The responsibilities of the media and paranormal claims. *Skeptical Inquirer.* 1985.

Lewis, Chad. *Investigating Students' Belief in the Paranormal.* Master's Thesis. 2002

Pepin County Press 8 September, 1860.

Sparks, G.G., C.L. Nelson, and R.G. Campbell. (1997). "The Relationship Between

Exposure to Televised Messages About Paranormal Phenomena and Paranormal

Beliefs." *Journal of Broadcasting & Electronic Media* 41. 1997.

Chapter 12. Is Pepie a Hoax?

Lewis, Chad. *Hidden Headlines of Wisconsin.* Eau Claire: On the Road Publications. 2007.

Lewis, Chad. *The Wisconsin Road Guide to Mysterious Creatures.* Eau Claire: On the Road Publications. 2011.

Chapter 13. Cryptozoological Potentials

Beveridge, William I.B. The Art of Scientific Investigation. Blackburn Press, 2004.

Cohen, Morris F. An Introduction To Logic And Scientific Method. Hughes Press, 2008.

Coleman, Loren. Cryptozoology A To Z: The Encycolopedia of Loch Monsters, Sasquatch, Chupacabras, and Other Authentic Mysteries of Nature. Touchstone, 1999.

Kaku, Michio. Hyperspace: A Scientific Odyssey Through Parallel Universes, Time Warps, and the 10th Dimension. Anchor, 1995.

Keel, John A. The Mothman Prophesies. New York, NY: Tor, 1991.

Kelleher, Colm A. and George Knapp. Hunt for the Skinwalker. New York, NY: Pocket Books, 2005.

Talbot, Michael. The Holographic Universe. New York, NY: Harper Collins, 1991.

Vallee, Jacques. Passport to Magonia: From Folklore to Flying Saucers. Chicago, IL: Henry Regnery Company, 1969.

Chapter 14. UFO Sightings & Alien Connections

Above Top Secret. "UFO Crash Event: Shag Harbor, 1967." Accessed 2014. http://www.abovetopsecret.com/forum/thread485206

Hickson, Charles and Mendez, William. UFO Contact at Pascagoula. Wendel C Stevens Publishing, 1983.

Lapseritis, Jack. Interview by Noah Voss. Phone. 2007.

Lapseritis, Jack. The Psychic Sasquatch: And Their UFO Connection. Blue Water Publishing, 1998.

MUFON. "Minnesota UFO Sightings." Accessed 2014. http://www.mufon.com

MUFON. "Wisconsin UFO Sightings." Accessed 2014. http://www.mufon.com

NUFORC. "Minnesota UFO Sightings." Accessed 2014. http://www.nuforc.org

NUFORC. "Wisconsin UFO Sightings." Accessed 2014. http://www.nuforc.org

Smith, Warren. Strange Monsters and Madmen. Popular Library, New York, 1969

Steiger, Brad. Interview by Noah Voss. Email. 2007, 2012, 2014.

UFO Casebook. "The 1967 Shag Harbor UFO Crash." Accessed 2014. http://www.ufocasebook.com/Shagharbor.html

UFO Wisconsin "Wisconsin UFO Sightings." Accessed 2014. http://UFOwisconsin.com

Voss, Noah. UFO Wisconsin – A Progress Report. Unexplained Research Publishing, 2008.

Keep your adventure going with *The Van Meter Visitor!*

www.thevanmetervisitor.com